Acknowledgements

Rose Pettengell gave the manuscript
and graced me with timely en~
forward to reading her books
beating in her thinking heart
honour British English ov~   ~.

    Krystal Cates ha~   corner
for twenty-two years, savi~,   doubtful
soul with her generous heart, ~.   ~er criticism.
She is, to my mind, the only true ~   ~ in Texas.

Kevin Cole and I had so many discussions about
Shakespeare and tragedy that I scarcely know where his
mind trails off and my begins.

Richard Begam always believed I could write
and publish something unacademic and apparently he's
right. His loyalty and friendship have kept me above
ground.

Cal Hewitt and Henry Baxter made valuable
eleventh-hour suggestions and have the literary
judgement of which one dreams but never expects in
people so young.

I am grateful for my fiancée's love of Hyde
Park, where serendipity smiled on me in the form of a
brief encounter with Jacob Lewis, my new editor,
who—along with his mother, Elsa Lewis—took a
chance on my gloomy little Dane so that he might
venture out to see the world.

My faithful nephew, Jason Yohe, stayed on
board for many years and is responsible for the
illustration of Hamlet at Yorick's gravesite, an image so
perfect that I do in fact want this book to be judged by
its cover.

*For my nieces and nephews and their children
and for all the lonely, brainy Hamlets out there*

Contents

"Yorick is both Hamlet's true mother and his father."

Harold Bloom

A Game of Ice-Chess

"At last, Prince Hamlet!" exclaimed Yorick when he finally discovered the boy shivering on the ground and resting his back against a stone slab in the graveyard. Although the trees, bushes, and tombstones were covered in a thick hoar-frost, Hamlet gave no thought to the cold, preferring to be alone to have intellectual debates with himself. He had so many hiding places that it was becoming harder and harder for anyone to find him, and even his beloved friend, who was also the court jester, sometimes had to search for hours to locate the elusive Prince of Denmark. This time he found Hamlet in the graveyard hiding behind the tombstone of an ancient King. The boy said he liked to sit with the dead. He claimed they calmed his nerves. Yes, of course death was depressing. But living people could be such hard work. Locked in their silent tombs or planted in the frozen earth, the dead were not much trouble anymore.

"Yorick!" shouted the Prince, delighted to see his endlessly-animated best friend. The boy scrambled to his feet and the two exchanged a bear hug. Yorick had become a second father to Hamlet. His own father spent most of his time on affairs of state, either killing foreign invaders or expanding his kingdom. Yorick stayed home and told jokes.

Like most jesters, Yorick's head was shaved and it sloped down to ginger-red eyebrows that were so bushy sparrows could have nested in them. His shining blue eyes were full of laughter. Yorick was hefty but not exactly fat and he wore some of the colourful and showy clothes expected of court jesters, but he refused to wear the ridiculous hat with the three bells on it. Yorick told the King and court that their laughter would be his jingle bells. He loved two things in his life: eating and talking to Hamlet. Having no family of his own, Yorick had taken Hamlet under his wing and taught him about the wisdom of fools. The King and Queen were often worried that Hamlet spent too much time with Yorick but the Prince found the jester excellent company and a superior teacher of puns. Yorick encouraged the boy to play with language, not always to the amusement of those around him.

Although Hamlet had much to live for, he spent most of his time alone, thinking about everything under the stars but especially about why he was so full of complicated thoughts that would keep him up half the night. And every day he wondered, "Why does my mind feel like both a trusted friend AND my worst enemy?" But the boy could never figure it out. The Prince had Viking ancestors who were so manly they had to shave their beards between meals, but Hamlet saw little in himself to resemble the former lions of his blood. He was small for his age, his skin was yellowish and pale like autumn moonlight, and his hair looked like a mop had been dipped in a bucket of ink and flung over his head. Hamlet had ice-blue eyes that were both penetrating and melancholic, both bright and brooding. His clothes were wearing him rather than the other way around but Hamlet did not care that his courtly costumes were often too big for him to fill. The Prince's small hands were white and bony. When he was excited, they would take flight like startled seagulls.

Yorick rested his hand on the icy tombstone Hamlet had been hiding behind.

"Had enough of the dead for one day?" he asked.

Yorick was the only person in Denmark who did not think Hamlet's obsession with death was unusual or disturbing. He thought it made the lad more interesting and actually improved his sense of humour.

"To be honest, I am a little tired of being grave today," said the boy.

"All this thinking will make you a philosopher one day," replied Yorick.

"But I am to be *King* one day," said Hamlet, "not a *philosopher*."

"Why not be *both* a philosopher and a King at once?" suggested Yorick.

"Because philosophers do nothing but think all day and do not have time to rule a kingdom. Father says I think things to death and—when I stop to think about it—sometimes I think he's right," said Hamlet.

"That may be true," said Yorick, "but isn't it best to be as wise as a philosopher and also to rule as a good King?"

"I will have to think more about that," said Hamlet, "but why did you seek me out?"

"Game of chess?" said Yorick.

"Excellent idea!" replied Hamlet cheerfully.

"And on this occasion, I have a surprise for you."

"Oh, tell me *now*!"

"Patience, Prince."

The jester and the boy left the graveyard and made the journey back to the castle at Elsinore, chatting the entire way and making puns and riddles for each other. Yorick was the first to fling a riddle at Hamlet.

"What makes pawns angry?"

Hamlet pondered the question for a few moments but had to give up.

"Always being pushed around" said Yorick.

As they approached the castle, a rabbit raced across their paths and disappeared into the woods nearby. Hamlet slowly said, "That rabbit *rabbited* far too quickly for me!" Yorick saw his opening, and replied, "Hare one minute—gone the next!" Hamlet groaned an appreciative groan, which was good enough for the court jester. Yorick noticed Hamlet's pace slowing and wondered if the lad were getting weary from walking, for the Prince was not the most robust boy in Denmark.

"Shall I carry you on my back?" asked Yorick.

When Hamlet was younger, Yorick used to bear him on his back many times to help get the Prince home to the castle in a timely way.

"Am I not a bit old for that, now?" replied

Hamlet. He was a little embarrassed because in fact he *was* tired and loved his piggy-back rides with Yorick.

"Maybe just one more time," said Yorick cheerfully, and he fell to his knees so Hamlet could scramble aboard Yorick's broad back. Hamlet was in a position to see over Yorick's head as they made their way along the path. After a minute or two, Hamlet fondly patted Yorick on his bald head and said:

"Alas—poor Yorick—has to carry a Prince, heavy with thoughts, all the way home."

"Your thoughts," exclaimed Yorick, "weigh much more than you do!"

Hamlet pondered this thought as Yorick made his way home. Suddenly, the Prince said:

"Yorick, I have just thought of something else!"

"You do seem a bit heavier all of a sudden," said Yorick. "What is your new thought?"

"The weight of thoughts," replied Hamlet, "makes one delay doing anything."

"That's true, young Prince," said Yorick.

"In other words," Hamlet said, "mental weight makes one *wait*..."

Yorick smiled.

"Now *that*," he said to the boy on his back, "is a *weighty* thought!"

Hamlet found himself drumming his fingers

on Yorick's big skull and giggling how easily the court jester and he could play with words.

After another half-an-hour, the two reached the castle and immediately went into the Great Hall to warm themselves by a hearth always banked with glowing logs. After a minute of clapping their hands and stomping their feet, Yorick said:

"I'll fetch the board." Yorick seemed strangely excited and was gone for longer than was necessary, for the chess set was stored in a room not far from the Great Hall. Yorick had first taught the Prince how to play chess and, despite his love for him, the jester would often grow impatient when it took Hamlet so long to make a move. In the tangle of his mind Hamlet found it difficult to know what to do, which piece to move, and when. And he wondered why winning the game was more important than the elegant dance of the pieces.

As Hamlet became an experienced player, he actually made his moves *more* slowly. Sometimes he would delay making a move for an entire hour, during which time the court jester would hum ballads, inhale roasted chickens, dance jigs, comb his unruly eyebrows, or juggle legs of lamb. Yorick would sometimes gently chide the Prince on his indecision and even call Hamlet 'The Prince of Procrastination.' Hamlet did not like this name and considered himself more a 'Prince of Deliberation.' He had immense difficulty in moving his queen and, when she was captured, Hamlet would cry out as if he had been stabbed.

Yorick finally returned with the chess board and a green velvet pouch containing the chess pieces.

He waved Hamlet over to the enormous, oak table in the centre of the Hall. Sitting across from Hamlet, he put the chess board on the table and spilt the bag of pieces. But this was not their usual set carved from bone (an earlier birthday gift for Hamlet). They were glassy pieces covered in frost.

"We must be quick," said Yorick.

"Where did you get these odd pieces?" asked the Prince.

Yorick beamed with pleasure.

"Yesterday I sat outside in my heavy coat for several hours and carved the entire set from pieces of ice. I found frozen muddy water to make the darker pieces. Now we must play before they melt!" The Prince was pleased but vexed by Yorick's ingenuity. Together the boy and the jester set up the board, Hamlet playing black, as usual, and handling with special care his little ice-queen as he placed her on her square.

Yorick immediately pushed a chilly pawn two squares forward. At first, Hamlet waited several minutes to move but when he saw the little pieces forming tiny puddles, he picked up speed. He was especially alarmed to see his ice-queen lose her features and watch her tiny crown melting. But he could also not bear to move too quickly and he agonised over the fate of the pieces as he deployed them. Hamlet had to think quickly and act quickly and that agitated him. After about ten minutes of play in front of a blazing fireplace, Yorick took Hamlet's ice-queen while she was still recognisable. Hamlet gloomily watched Yorick snatch up his little, melting queen and put her among the other captured pieces collectively forming a kind of lumpy iceberg on the table where the two played.

Finally, Yorick's translucent queen skated over to Hamlet's dark ice-king and the game was over. A frustrated Hamlet tipped over his king to show he had been check-mated.

"Well, what did you think of our game?" asked Yorick.

"It was really unnerving! And there's something sad about all the pieces melting into one puddle."

"'Tis true," agreed Yorick, "but life does go by quickly and I am afraid that King Death is the only King that does not get check-mated."

Hamlet fell into one of his long silences and finally said,

"Yorick, what happens to us when we melt?"

"Many think we go to heaven or hell or someplace in-between but I have my doubts. What do you think, young Prince?"

"I see dead animals all the time. They rot on the ground and insects feast on them. It looks as if they simply don't exist anymore. But the Church teaches us of an afterlife. Is there an afterlife or is that just a fairytale?"

"There is an afterlife if you *think* there is," observed Yorick.

"But what is the truth about the afterlife?"

"Maybe the truth is only what you *think* it is."

Hamlet simply stared at Yorick's cheerful, wise eyes and took on board this difficult thought. After a long pause, Hamlet said, very sadly, "I sometimes think my mind is not my friend. Thinking usually confuses and depresses me."

Yorick got up from the table and went around to Hamlet and ruffled his mop of hair. He then pulled back, looked at him and gently said, "You are sad and confused all the time because you are very, very *intelligent*."

Hamlet had to think about that, too, but it was time to move on.

"At the end of the game," the Prince said, "the king and the pawn go into the same box."

Yorick smiled warmly and replied, "Or the same puddle."

"A great teacher and jester has finally taught me how to move more quickly."

Yorick put his hand on the Prince's shoulder and said:

"*Chess-mate!*"

Hamlet's laughter echoed throughout the room. The two walked out of the Great Hall together and the Prince wondered if he would ever have a truer friendship. On the table the chess pieces slowly melted into the table and then disappeared altogether.

S/words

few days after his chess game with Yorick, Hamlet wandered into the Great Hall of the castle at Elsinore where he found his father the King, his mother the Queen, his Uncle Claudius, and the King's chief counsellor, a man called Polonius, who Hamlet thought was too much in love with the sound of his own voice. They were seated at a large table discussing the political situation of Denmark when Prince Hamlet planted himself before them. The Queen gave her son a loving look that made his eyes widen. As Hamlet waited politely for a break in their conversation, he stared at the enormous bear rug at his feet. The King had killed the bear years ago. Its massive jaws were open, as if in a permanent roar, and its long, yellowing canine teeth still looked deadly. Hamlet gazed at the splayed out legs and claws, each set of claws pointing to a cardinal point on a map. One bear claw was reaching North, pointing straight at Hamlet. He thought to himself: *'Tis to give me a true bearing.* Since the court jester was not around, he kept the pun to himself.

Finally, there was a pause in the discussion and Hamlet ventured an announcement:

"I have been having some bad dreams but Yorick has helped me to understand them."

The King frowned and stroked his dark, sable beard. He was not in favour of Hamlet's having bad dreams.

Hamlet's mother, the Queen, was first to reply.

"My poor young Prince! You perhaps spend too much time with that man and his silly theories and jokes."

Before Hamlet could speak up to defend Yorick, the King broke in.

"You will one day be King of Denmark. *That* is something worth dreaming about."

"Those kinds of dreams," replied the Prince, "are like ambitions and are conscious. I have those dreams, too. But at night I have no control over my dreams. Anything can happen. Last night I dreamt about a dragon in the orchard, and…"

Before Hamlet could go on, Polonius cut him off and addressed them all.

"The young Prince sometimes seems too clever for his own good. He would rather play with *words* than with *swords*. My son, Laertes, would like to practise fencing with your son but he is never to be found except in some nook reading his books or wandering all over the kingdom with that absurd jester."

"*Words* rather than *swords*," said Hamlet dreamily, "that's excellent." Hamlet loved to see how little it took to make one word turn into another word, or in this case into a sword. At this point, Uncle Claudius felt he should say something.

"My young nephew is clearly clever, but it takes action, not merely words, to run a kingdom. Perhaps he should read less and act more like the

Prince he is."

Before the Queen could interject, Hamlet quickly replied.

"I see no reason why a good ruler cannot be good with both words and swords. Surely a good king has to know how to make speeches and compose treaties and that sort of thing."

The King now spoke up.

"What you say is true, my son, but you should not neglect the fact that you must go out and conquer foreign lands and expand the kingdom. That is a matter of *deeds*, not *words*."

"With respect," replied Hamlet, shakily facing his father, "I sometimes wonder why Denmark needs to be any bigger than it already is. I can ride my horse for hours and hours and not reach the end of it."

The King, the Queen, Claudius, and Polonius all looked at one another. That was not the kind of thing a future King should say or even think. And whenever Hamlet began a sentence with the words "with respect" he usually meant "with no respect" and then went on to say something completely disrespectful.

"One day," said the King, "I shall have to go to Norway and fight a war there against a King called Fortinbras. If I win, we can gain territory and enrich our kingdom. One day, you too will have to go to war to gain more land for Denmark. That's how the world works."

Hamlet pondered this thought. He did not want to upset his father and the court but he also could not understand why Denmark needed to be any larger than it was. And he pondered the name 'Fortinbras' – it meant 'strong arm.' Hamlet wondered why having a strong mind was not better than having a strong arm. Hamlet tried one more time to press his point.

"But why can't I enlarge *my mind* as well as enlarge the kingdom? Yorick says…"

At this point, Uncle Claudius rudely interrupted the Prince.

"Yorick is paid to be a fool and say foolish things. You would do well to spend less time with Yorick and more time learning how to be a good King."

"But what *is* a good king?" asked Hamlet, innocently. He really wanted to know.

The Queen took this opportunity to say:

"Your father is a good King. He is wise, judicious and powerful. And he knows how to conquer neighbouring kingdoms when the time is right."

The King and Queen exchanged what seemed to be loving looks.

Some neighbour, Hamlet thought, but he merely stared at the cold, stony floor of the Great Hall and kept his thoughts to himself. He looked so sad and pensive that the Queen came over to him and put her arms around him.

"My little Prince," she said gently, pressing the side of his head to her ample bosom, "Why must you think everything into a dark corner? You must know it is common for the Prince to rule the kingdom one day. And the best kingdom is the largest one. Surely you can see that."

Still preferring a large mind over a large kingdom, Hamlet was about to reply but decided it was fruitless and so he fell silent and allowed his beautiful mother to hug him tightly. At such moments he felt the warmth of her uncomplicated love and the world made sense to him. The men looked at the Queen and Prince Hamlet with varying degrees of disapproval. Uncle Claudius looked, particularly unhappy at mother and son being so closely bonded. Polonius, who always felt he had to say something, decided to speak up once more to gain young Hamlet's attention.

"My Lord Hamlet—I know where you can find my son, Laertes. I shall give you directions. Why don't you go and seek him out and practise fencing? He is excessively eager to enjoin your respective talents in what doubtless will be a superlatively precocious match." The Prince found Polonius's idea tiresome and wondered if Polonius were getting paid by the syllable. He liked Laertes well enough but vastly preferred the company of Laertes' clever and enchanting sister, Ophelia.

"That's an excellent idea," agreed Claudius, "Laertes is keen to improve his swordsmanship and you look like you could use some physical exercise."

Hamlet gloomily pried himself away from his mother, and said:

"Very well, but I prefer *wordsmanship* to swordsmanship."

Polonius pounced on this remark.

"'Wordsmanship' is not a word, my lord. You cannot simply make up words."

"Why ever not?" asked Hamlet, and continued, "Are not all words made up? And if we don't make them up, *then who will?*"

The four adults in the Great Hall stared helplessly at one another. What could they say?

Finally, the King decided to make a pronouncement.

"You cannot," he told his son, "simply go around making up words. What if everyone went around making up words all the time? What kind of world would *that* be?"

Hamlet pulled away from his mother, took three steps backwards and suddenly let his hands take wing as he threw them in the air:

"It would be the world *we live in now*! But now I must seek out Laertes and put an edge on his swordsmanship."

Hamlet left the Great Hall and none of the four adults had the faintest clue what was really going on inside his boyish skull. Hamlet did not seek out Laertes for a sweaty bout of sword-play. Instead, he decided to hole up for a few hours in one of his favourite hiding places in the castle, a place stuffed with books that he piled up and used as fortifications of his own. As he clambered into his secret reading nook and assembled his private castle of books, Hamlet thought to himself how much he enjoyed being encastled behind words and avoiding the ridiculous world where adults seem to do nothing but get upset over politics and how to make the kingdom as vast as possible. Every night you go to bed wanting more and each day simply brings you closer to your grave-- a little hole in the ground, a parody of empire.

The Prince pulled one volume from his wall of books and curled up to read. He knew the opening words by heart.

Sing, Goddess, Achilles' rage,

Black and murderous, that cost the Greeks

Incalculable pain, pitched countless souls

Of heroes into Hades' dark,

And left their bodies to rot as feasts.

For dogs and birds, as Zeus' will was done.

Hamlet could never figure out if Homer were *praising* or *blaming* Achilles, the great Greek hero of the Trojan War. His fellow Greeks certainly had something to complain about. Hamlet's final reflection for the day was that words were better than swords. But it was a thought that he had to keep to himself. He was beginning to think that his castle of books was kingdom enough for him.

At the Reflecting Pond

Prince Hamlet sat in his secret sanctuary, a heavy book cradled in his arms. Only a small handful of people knew where to find him, including Ophelia, the daughter of Polonius. Although Ophelia was not as high-born as Hamlet, the two had spent enough time together to become fast friends. In the wide-moated fortress of his mind, Hamlet lowered the drawbridge for few, but she was among them. Ophelia had silken, light-brown hair and her eyes were the colour of a deep-blue sky during a dying day. Hamlet called them "twilight eyes." Rightly suspecting he was in his reading nook, Ophelia sought him out there and quietly approached Hamlet, hoping not to surprise or disturb him too much.

"What are you reading?" enquired Ophelia, tip-toeing into his chamber.

Hamlet looked up from his book.

"Words—mostly nouns, some adjectives—a few articles," he replied.

"No verbs?"

"I am not too keen on verbs. I think I might go to school in Germany."

"Why Germany?" asked Ophelia.

"Because in Germany the verbs are banished to the end of the sentence. I like to delay the verbs, or rather the verbs I like to delay."

"Why is that?"

"Verbs make me feel like I should be *doing* something."

"What's wrong with doing something?"

"Doing things keeps me from reading—and thinking."

"You *are* something of a bookworm. But what I meant was: what is *the subject* of your book?"

"It's a book about perfidious princes."

"'Perfidious'…that means 'treacherous', does it not?"

"Yes, it does. It seems all princes must be perfidious to be good at their jobs."

"Do you like the book? You seem a bit gloomy."

"The subject is a prince but a Prince is *not a subject*."

"What do you mean?" asked Ophelia.

"I mean that Princes and Queens and Kings are *not subject* to anyone, and therefore are not *subjects*."

"Sometimes you baffle me," said Ophelia.

"I often baffle myself," replied Hamlet.

To brighten up the mood, Ophelia hit on an idea.

"This is awfully serious talk. We should continue it at the Reflecting Pond!"

"Brilliant idea! Let's go at once," exclaimed a suddenly animated Hamlet.

Ever since they were small children and had discovered a secluded pond not too far from the castle, Hamlet and Ophelia would go there to be alone and talk to each other about anything that occurred to them. It was their own secret hiding place from the rituals and routines of courtly life and the frequent, unwanted interference from adults. They cherished their time at what they called the 'Reflecting Pond.' For in that pond they could see their images as they talked and offered each other their reflections about everything in the world. A large willow tree stood next to the pond, the tips of its sweeping branches gently stroking the water. Beneath its shimmering surface, the pond was dangerously deep.

As they walked to the pond they crossed a meadow filled with wildflowers of all kinds. Ophelia began picking pansies as they strolled and she started to weave them into a circle.

"What are you doing?" inquired Hamlet.

"Since you are not subject to anyone and will one day be King of Denmark, I thought I would make a crown for you to wear so you can get used to the idea."

"Splendid!" said Hamlet. He also began to gather wild daisies to do the same thing for Ophelia, fancying her his Queen.

That one day they both might be King and Queen was a day-dream they shared, although Ophelia had heard that Hamlet would probably have to marry some Norwegian Princess. "It's all about politics, not love," she thought, and Hamlet tended to agree with her. He had built a nest for Ophelia in his heart. But they both suspected they would never be able to live as husband and wife, and it broke their young hearts. They seemed to have so much in common and, despite often being sadly contemplative, they also both snorted and giggled at the same things, and their laughter was a kind of blooming love.

By the time they reached the reflecting pond they had completed their tasks and they each put a natural crown on the other's head, as if it were a solemn ceremony. Ophelia looked very pretty indeed, Hamlet thought, with her crown of daisies, and Hamlet—so Ophelia thought—looked very appropriate wearing his small hoop of pansies.

"A thought just occurred to me," said Hamlet.

"Well, you've come to the right place!" said Ophelia as they neared the Reflecting Pond.

"The crown you've given me is a kind of thinking cap."

"As if you need one!"

"What I mean is this, said Hamlet, the word 'pansy' comes from the French word *pensée*, which refers to thoughts. Pansies have sad little drooping faces because thoughts often make one sad. Here is a simile: 'as sad as a pansy.'"

"Oh, I see," said Ophelia, "and so your simile is also a repetition."

Hamlet pondered this. He marvelled at the telepathy he had developed with Ophelia.

"That is exactly so, Ophelia. 'Sad as a pansy' is really saying the same thing twice. But I wonder if being a 'Pansy-King' is also a kind of contradiction, now that I think about it."

"What do you mean?"

"My father and uncle say I think too much to get anything important done. Kings must be aggressive Verbs, not ponderous Nouns. But Yorick believes that there is no contradiction between being full of thoughts and being a good King. Yorick would say that the Pansy-Prince might grow up to be the Philosopher-King."

Ophelia thought about that idea for a few minutes. And unlike anyone he knew except for Yorick, she replied with a probing question.

"But what do *you* think?"

Hamlet fell silent for two minutes during which time he and Ophelia slowly circled each other around the pond, their eyes holding each other in a distant but intense embrace. Finally, Hamlet spoke up.

"As with so many other things, I am of two minds. Actually, I am of *four* minds. And they don't agree on anything. They are a quartet out of tune."

From the other side of the pond, Ophelia considered his reply for a moment and then suddenly said, "Reflection Time!" This was another little ritual they had created over the years. It meant that they both had to fall to their knees on the edge of the pond, be silent and contemplate their own images in the still water. The two thinkers immediately and dramatically collapsed to lean over the pond, watching their reflections come into focus. After a few moments Ophelia's hand went up to touch her crown of daisies and she saw a hand in the pond do the same thing. She watched a mirrored smile appear in the green water. Hamlet inspected his own image in the pond and noticed for the hundredth time how pensive he looked. Suddenly the crown of pansies fell from his head into the pond and he saw his reflection from within the crown, whose fall agitated the calm surface and sent out widening concentric circles, like expanding haloes around his head.

"All my reflections are wobbly!" cried out Hamlet and, in reaching out to retrieve his lost crown, he fell headlong into the pond.

Not knowing how to swim, he began thrashing about but almost instantly started sinking into the unknown depths. Neither he nor Ophelia had actually been swimming in the pond and had no idea what lurked beneath the surface or exactly how deep it was. They both thought that the still surface reflecting their thoughts was dangerous enough. But now the Prince of Denmark was gone and Ophelia instantly threw herself into the water, reaching for any touch of Hamlet near the spot where he had disappeared. As for Hamlet, after the shock of immersion and the panic about not knowing how to swim, he held his breath for a moment but then felt a strange calm in letting go. The water was cool and slippery. He felt his sinking limbs splay like the bear rug in the Great Hall. Was this what it felt like to die? It might not be so bad after all. But just as Hamlet was about to inhale his first breath of pond water, a frantic hand somehow found the front of his shirt, seized it, and began dragging the boy towards the surface. Hamlet did not struggle against the force. He had no idea it was Ophelia trying to rescue him. Both his mind and body had gone slack. Once on the surface, Ophelia kept one hand on Hamlet's shirt and paddled with her other arm to the edge of the pond. It was an awkward manoeuvre for them both but in a few moments Ophelia had managed to lug the Prince to the edge and he crawled slowly up the steep bank. Ophelia followed him and they both lay side by side, breathing heavily for several minutes, the young Prince coughing and spitting.

When Hamlet had recovered, he propped himself up on his elbow and stared at Ophelia.

"You saved my life!"

The girl said nothing but looked at young Hamlet through her tangled hair and she thought he had never looked so alive. A great love crested and without knowing how or why Ophelia began to cry. For once in his life, Hamlet was speechless. His face was more pensive than ever but in his surging soul he knew he had fallen in love with Ophelia and that one day he wanted to be her husband, no matter what the obstacles. He reached over and with a delicate finger moved a few locks of her wet hair aside so he could see her blue eyes better. Ophelia was still quietly weeping because she was so happy to have him safe and by her side. If Hamlet looked closely he could see a tiny image of himself in the pools of her eyes. It was another game they used to play. But now he saw only Ophelia. And for a flicker he forgot the impossibility of their love.

"Leave the weeping to the willow," said Hamlet, nodding to the branches above them. A slow smile crept across Ophelia's face. It was like something Yorick would say, she thought.

They looked back at the pond. The flowers of their two crowns had scattered and mixed together, decorating the surface of the water which was still trembling from the tumult of their splash.

The Prince and Ophelia picked themselves up and laughed at each other's soaked clothing. And then, for the first time and without giving it a thought, they walked hand–in–hand through the wildflowers back to the castle, their hearts light and their clothes drying patchily under a struggling autumn sun. On their short journey home, Ophelia sang a song she had composed for Hamlet. Her voice went up and down in a way Hamlet found enchanting.

"Never a Viking, Hamlet"

Life is too short for long faces –

Yet lost in his endless mind

A most melancholy young Prince

Finds no one of his kind.

Never a Viking, Hamlet --

No, never a Viking, he.

Never a Viking, Hamlet --

A Prince of Mortality.

He has a princedom to wander –

A kingdom soon to rule,

But he follows his vagrant thoughts,
A truly wise young fool.
Never a Viking, Hamlet--
No, never a Viking, he.
Never a Viking, Hamlet –
A Prince of Mortality.

Above the black, churning sea
He contemplates his death,
The highest of all animals
Sadly he draws his breath.

Never a Viking, Hamlet --
No, never a Viking, he.
Never a Viking, Hamlet --
A Prince of Mortality.

A pilgrim in his sleepless soul
He journeys into night
To find more thoughts to contemplate
Until he mourns the light.

Never a Viking, Hamlet --
No, never a Viking, he.
Never a Viking, Hamlet --

A Prince of Mortality –

A Prince of Mortality.

They sang the song several times. Before long they reached the darkening castle just as the brooding blue twilight turned the colour of Ophelia's eyes.

Bear

The fact that Hamlet was growing into someone not at all like his Viking ancestors was not lost on the King or his Uncle Claudius. What Ophelia had turned into a pretty song was based on the truth: Hamlet *was* turning into a Prince of Contemplation rather than a Prince of Action. Concerned that Prince Hamlet might not be up to his future role, the King and ~~Uncle~~ Claudius decided to take him on a bear hunt to see if the boy could at least be trusted to kill wild animals, which is what any self-respecting Prince must be able to do. Hamlet would have preferred to read in his castle of books, play ice-chess with Yorick, wander with Ophelia or do almost anything with his mother, but he had no choice but to play the part of the hunter for a few days.

~~One~~ on a bright, cold morning, the King, Claudius and the Prince set out on horseback to the forest to hunt for bear. In attendance were the usual band of huntsmen with their bows and arrows, spears, dogs, tents and usual trappings for a royal hunt. The entourage spent three days hunting deer and boar but Hamlet was meant to observe and wait for his chance for a bear. On the fourth day of the hunt, the King and Claudius told Hamlet that today just the three of them would set out for a bear hunt. They were going into the forest on foot and not take the dogs or any other help. This was clearly some kind of test of Hamlet's Danish manhood. The Prince would have preferred a vocabulary quiz.

As they walked into the lush, green forest, Hamlet felt the need to say something.

"Why don't we hunt for unicorns?" he asked.

"Because they don't exist," objected his uncle Claudius, always mystified by the Prince's odd remarks.

"All the more reason," replied Hamlet, "to hunt them."

The King and Claudius looked at each other as if to say, "what are we going *to* do with this lad?"

"No, no, no," said King Hamlet, "we must follow the spoor of a great bear and have you kill it and bring it home to roast." By 'spoor,' the King meant bear excrement. And sure enough, after an hour of searching the floor of the forest, the King suddenly announced that he had discovered fresh bear faeces.

"Excellent!" said Claudius, "the hunt is on." The two men were excited. Prince Hamlet found it easy to contain *his* excitement.

As usual, Hamlet was thinking up a storm. What is the point, he asked himself, of bringing home a bear? Deer and elk were much better to eat. And bears are big, fierce animals that can kill you with one swipe of their paw. Hamlet knew he was being tested for his courage, but he thought it would be far more interesting to hunt down the spoor of an *idea* than the spoor of a bear. Ideas also leave tracks and sometimes bleed. Why not follow *that* spoor? Where does the idea of *nobility* come from, pondered Hamlet, now *that* is a spoor worth following. The entire hunting business and tracking down bear faeces began to make him cross.

"Bear spoor is a bore," said Hamlet, before he realised he had spoken and not just thought the words. And before he could stop his mind and mouth from working in concert, he also said, "Boar spore is *really* a bore."

"Well, boring or not, you are going to kill a bear today," snapped his father.

Hamlet thought: "I really cannot bear bear" but kept the pun to himself.

And so the three of them went deeper and deeper into the forest, Hamlet growing more fearful and gloomy with every step as the three of them followed bear droppings.

Hamlet knew the word 'spoor' had several related meanings in Danish and that pleased him. So while the King and his brother were concerned to find a trail of bear faeces, Hamlet followed the spoor of etymology, tracing words through the forest of derivations to see where the scent led him. *Spoor*, thought Hamlet, can refer to the track or trail or scent that an animal leaves behind. It can also mean a trace or vestige or mark. Most exciting of all, a spoor could be a *clue*, or a lead. Hamlet tried to imagine the bear hunt was a kind of detective game and that the bear was really some kind of fugitive or phantom eluding their pursuit. If the animal is wounded it becomes much easier to track because it leaves behind a blood-spoor and you just have to follow the blood, which was easy for a good Viking.

But *am* I a good Viking? wondered the Prince. As with so many other things, he had his doubts. His Danish ancestors haunted him and sometimes he thought it was unfair to have to be a pagan warrior for the rest of his life just because he was born with a certain name in a certain country in a certain time. And besides, thought Hamlet, the Danish Vikings had their heyday of pillaging and marauding and mayhem a few centuries earlier. Why go on with these customs? Isn't it best sometimes to break away from certain practices and traditions in order to grow up? All these interesting thoughts were racing around in Hamlet's mind as he pretended to be fascinated by bear excrement. It occurred to the Prince that the word 'poo' was lurking pungently inside the word 'spoor' but he did not think the stern King and his unsmiling uncle Claudius would be at all amused or interested in that coincidence. To divert himself he began humming the chorus from Ophelia's song and thought that he would have made a very unspectacular Viking.

After five hours of tracking the bear, the King announced that they must be getting close and to keep their bows and arrows ready for instant action. The idea of instant action made the Prince a little sick to his stomach. But he readied his bow and selected an arrow, although his nervous hands were already shaking. After another half-an-hour, the King signalled to Claudius and the Prince that he had spotted their prey. He called Hamlet to his side and, when the boy was crouching next to him, said to his son, "There he is."

Hamlet peered through the trees and saw a large brown bear about forty feet away on his hind legs, sniffing the air, facing the hunters.

"Don't make a move," whispered the King.

"Don't worry," whimpered Hamlet, almost too terrified even to *look* at the bear.

The King waved Claudius off to one side so the three of them were not so bunched up. Then the King said to Hamlet, "Very slowly draw your bow and wait for the bear to turn. You need his broadside. You know where to aim, right?" The Prince had been coached during target practice to shoot just above and behind the forelegs of a bear, slightly from rear, to try to hit both the heart and lungs, if possible.

"Yes, I know," whispered Hamlet, "the beating heart, the breathing lungs, the source of all its life, its bear essentials."

"Shhhhh!" said the King, "No time for philosophy."

The bear was down on all fours and in position for the shot.

"Now," said the King.

A very miserable Prince got to his feet and felt all his blood draining like ice water into his legs. He pulled back the bow and began to wonder about the word 'bear' and where it came from.

"Now!" whispered the King with great vehemence.

The bear began to walk as Hamlet's wobbly hands released the arrow. It raced straight into the bear's buttock. The bear's roar filled up the entire forest.

A few feet away to the side, Uncle Claudius was the first to speak and said with withering sarcasm: Well done, boy!"

Before Hamlet could say anything the three
were running like mad through the woods, for the bear
had already begun its pursuit of them and there was no
time for the two men to launch even one arrow against
their furious pursuer. Now the hunters were the hunted
and Vikings are not especially fond of running away.
Prince Hamlet, however, was happy to turn tail and run
as fast as he could and yet he still had time to think.
His first thought was that he was sorry for hurting the
bear and how awful it must be to have an arrow lodged
in your back-side. He also wondered if the bear were a
mother who had any cubs about and, if so, how much
she would want to protect them, and how that would
only increase her anger. As Hamlet ran a few steps
ahead of the King and Claudius, he thought about a
bear's desire for revenge. Do bears have any concept
of revenge? Or was everything pure instinct? Can a
bear feel wronged? As Hamlet was contemplating
what a bear with a nasty arrow in its buttocks might be
thinking, the three runners found themselves at a broad
river and immediately they threw themselves in to
swim for the other side. Hamlet suddenly started
thrashing about because he recalled that he could not
swim. The King and Uncle Claudius grabbed the boy
and pulled him as they swam furiously to avoid the
bear, which had no trouble leaping into the river to
continue pursuing them. The two great Danes and the
not-so-great Dane reached the other side after a few
minutes of wild and clumsy swimming and then they
looked back across the river. The bear was making
steady headway towards them, the arrow sticking up in
the air like a skinny tail.

The King had his bow ready in an instant and
let fly an arrow, which hit the rear flank of the

swimming bear, and made it roar again but it did not stop swimming towards them.

Claudius gave the King a look of disdain, as if to say, "Am I the only one in this family that can shoot straight?"

But it was time to run again and after a few minutes of dashing through the woods with the bear in hobbled but enthusiastic pursuit, the Danes found themselves exhausted and each climbing a different tree in the hopes that the wounded bear would not be able to do any climbing with those two arrows sticking into it. It was not a sight anyone back in Elsinore would have believed: the King of Denmark, his brother Claudius and the Prince each twenty feet up his own oak tree. The bear bellowed its pain beneath them. Minutes passed.

The King was thinking of his absurd position up in the tree and was silently blaming the Prince for their predicament. He was also thinking about Gertrude and how eager he was to get back to her. And he was considering which kingdom needed conquering next. The King also wondered if his son would ever be a good killer. Uncle Claudius was also thinking about how absurd their position was and hoped that word would not get around how a wounded bear had pushed the three of them up trees. Claudius was also thinking of Gertrude, his sister-in-law, and wondered why Yorick looked at the Queen so oddly whenever he was making naughty jokes of one kind or another. What did that silly old fool *know*? Claudius also had a moment or two to consider his nephew's shaking hands and trouble using a bow and arrow. Would such a lad ever grow up to be a strong King?

Because Scandinavian countries preferred tanistry (succession based on the most able males of the blood) rather than primogeniture (first-born sons), Claudius sometimes wondered if *his* being the next King of Denmark were preferable if anything dire should befall his brother. What if the Prince were a coward or—what is worse—a clown?

For his part, Prince Hamlet was thinking about what animals think when you kill them, about what a noble brute his father was, about how strangely Uncle Claudius looked at him, about whether he would ever be a good killer and therefore a good king, about Ophelia back in the castle probably missing him (and how pretty and delicate her hands were), about what happens to us when we die, about the indifferent universe with its winking stars and unfathomable distances, and about the word 'unfathomable.' Hamlet was also thinking of his mother and wanted to run into her arms and be comforted. The bleeding bear howling below him was terrifying. Often when the Prince was scared or nervous, he began to play with words and he saw no reason why this occasion should be any different. The bear was going from one tree to the next, getting on its hind legs, and clawing at the bark two feet below each Dane while bellowing its rage. When it lumbered over to Prince Hamlet's tree and started its routine, the boy yelled down at the animal: "Bear with me!" The King and Claudius did not have a clue what Hamlet was intending but they suspected the Prince was not taking the situation as seriously as he should.

Suddenly, Claudius decided he had to do something, if only to stop Hamlet from further jesting. He found a way of sitting on a branch of his tree so he could draw his bow. It would not be a clean shot but the bear might run off if it were hit again. Claudius pulled the bow back and took aim at the bear's head. The arrow flew straight into the bear's ear. Stunned, the bear howled once again and Hamlet felt all his inner organs turn to slush. The badly-wounded bear reeled in circles before dashing away into the woods, no doubt to die in misery with three badly placed arrows sticking out of it.

"Can we go home now?" implored Prince Hamlet from his tree. The three Danes climbed down from their perches and the King said, "No, we must finish off the bear. It cannot go far and it is not humane to make it suffer in misery."

Hamlet thought that *not shooting* the bear in the first place was a good way to keep it from suffering but, as on so many other occasions, he kept his mouth shut. And so the three of them followed the blood spoor once more and eventually found the bear in the river they had earlier crossed. The bear looked as if it were trying to clean or numb its wounds in the rushing, cold water. The Prince felt terribly sorry for the bear but knew it had to die. Both the King and Claudius waded a little into the river, drew their bows and shot the bear at close range at the same time. Both arrows found their true home in the bear's heaving lungs. After one more exhausted roar of pain, the bear was silent. Its legs gave out and the strong current immediately swept the bear away. It looked like an island of fur that got smaller and smaller as it floated downstream.

"Can we go home now?" asked the Prince.

With nothing to show for their hunt, the King, Claudius and the Prince headed for the castle of Elsinore, avoiding the hunting party altogether. They made the long walk back in silence, each lost in his own thoughts, each regretting in different ways the episode with the bear. Prince Hamlet was a disappointment to both the King and his Uncle. But the two men could not know what a disappointment *they* were for the Prince. Hamlet usually idolised his father but, at times, when he stopped to think, he estimated that about half of the chores of being a man and being king were a little absurd. In his darker moments, when his mind was chased down by the most depressing thoughts, Hamlet thought that *life itself* was absurd. Kill the bear, don't kill the bear. What difference would it make in a hundred years? What difference would *anything* make in a hundred years? And then a truly devastating thought occurred to Hamlet: what difference does anything make *now*? The Prince knew these were dangerous thoughts, but he simply could not keep himself from hunting them down.

Dead Seagulls

A week after the failed hunting trip, Hamlet was taking one of his many solitary sea-strolls along the coast of Denmark. He liked listening to the cry of seagulls, to the sound of the crashing surf, and he enjoyed staring out at the straight line of the horizon. Hamlet often tried to clear his mind but he rarely had much success. There was simply too much to think about.

On this occasion, the Prince wandered down the coast until he happened upon two of his friends from school. They had rocks and slings and were knocking seagulls out of the sky. It was a little sport they enjoyed. Hamlet liked the boys for their wit and humour but sometimes he thought they were rather superficial. Their names were Rosencrantz and Guildenstern and they both came from noble families in Denmark. In a few years they were going to walk into piles of money and property. Even at the age of twelve, Rosencrantz and Guildenstern had nearly mastered the aristocratic art of doing absolutely nothing. They were dressed rather foppishly in shiny silks and their legs were clad in stockings of different colours. They each sported the latest fashion in lavish shirts—called 'doublets'—covered by smart, tight-fitting jackets called 'jerkins.' Although Rosencrantz and Guildenstern were dressed in different colours (lavender and saffron for the one, and emerald and pearl-grey for the other) it was remarkably difficult to tell them apart and people often confused their names, as if the two could be swapped around without anyone noticing.

As he approached the boys, Hamlet noticed that Rosencrantz had three dead seagulls at his feet. Guildenstern also had three. In order to keep the seagulls swooping and diving near them, the boys had put some food scraps in a pile on the beach. The gulls were very hungry and so took their chances. Hamlet did not approve of killing seagulls with rocks but he saw the pleasure it gave to his friends, so he did not make a fuss about it. Still, he thought that whacking birds out of the sky for fun was one of the most pointless things he could imagine. And baiting the hungry birds with a pile a food was not very sporting at all. There was something a bit underhanded about these two fellows.

'How now, lads!' shouted Hamlet.

The moment that Rosencrantz and Guildenstern saw the Prince of Denmark, they dropped their slings and ran over to hug him.

"My lord!" said Rosencrantz.

"My lord!" said Guildenstern.

They said this because strictly speaking their friend was also 'Lord Hamlet.' Hamlet and his two friends exchanged excited greetings and talked in idle ways about the goings-on at court.

"We looked around the castle before coming here," remarked Guildenstern, "thinking we might find you with Ophelia. But we had no luck so decided to go to the beach."

From time to time, the two boys liked to tease the Prince about Ophelia and his growing attraction to her.

"She's probably out climbing trees," said Rosencrantz.

"Well," said Hamlet, "she *does* go out on limb *in her mind*, but I'm not sure otherwise."

"Oh yes, she's always up some tree or other. She must be part squirrel," added Guildenstern, trying to be funny.

"Or just branching out" said Hamlet.

Rosencrantz and Guildenstern did not always understand Hamlet's wit or his puns and sometimes they thought he was trying too hard to be like Yorick.

After another ten minutes of banter, Guildenstern and Rosencrantz decided together that they were hungry and needed to return to Elsinore. They had one big empty stomach between them.

Hamlet sat down on the seashore and contemplated all the dead birds. The moment he left, he imagined that the other birds would descend to feed on the dead gulls, but not out of malice or for sport. Scavenger birds, thought Hamlet, are governed only by their stomachs, not unlike Rosencrantz and Guildenstern who were walking back to the castle for a snack.

Suddenly, without knowing why or thinking about it, Prince Hamlet began to cry. He was not mourning the death of the seagulls so much as the idiotic life of mankind, the cruelty and folly of his close friends, and the perfect indifference of the sun, the sea and the entire universe. What was important about the fall of a seagull? What was important about the fall of a Prince? Hamlet fell to his knees on the sand and felt a new kind of sadness that went beyond melancholy. Hamlet stared at the stunned, black, dead eyes of the seagulls, birds that a few minutes ago were darting and swooping and riding air currents. Now, they had ceased to exist. They were unseeing gulls. One day even young Ophelia's lucid, twilight eyes—a deeper royal blue—would darken and die. Why must everything beautiful die? What Hamlet was feeling was more than mourning. The Prince steadily wept, his small body quietly shuddering in despair. Hamlet wondered if anyone on the planet had ever experienced this new form of depression, fatigue, and loneliness. His entire body began to hurt as a vague but toxic sadness spread through him like eager cancer. He could hear the crazy laughter of Rosencrantz and Guildenstern in the distance. They were vibrant but vanishing smudges far down the beach, eventually becoming one patch of colour before becoming nothing.

And then out of nowhere a big hand clamped down on his shoulder. Hamlet had been so self-absorbed that he did not hear or see the person who had been almost running across the sand to get to him.

"How's my young Prince, then, not too well?"

"Yorick!" cried Hamlet.

The Prince scrambled to his feet. He and Yorick hugged each other tightly, the boy continuing to cry although he already felt better. He often thought that Yorick was both his true mother and his father.

"It seems Rosenstern and Guildencrantz have been here," said Yorick, looking at the dead seagulls.

The court jester was not too fond of the boys and
liked to mix up their names.

"Yes," replied Hamlet, "having absolutely
nothing to do, they thought they would kill things."

"Including *time*," observed Yorick.

Hamlet let Yorick's remark sink slowly into
his hurt heart. What could be worse than killing *time
itself*? Didn't time go by quickly enough without
having to kill it? Hamlet added that troubling thought
to the growing mountain of his doubts, his
meditations, his worries, and his aching sense that he
might not be cut out to be the Prince of Denmark.
Then it occurred to him how to summarise his
problems. He turned to Yorick and exclaimed:

"I don't have a stomach-ache or a tooth-ache
or a heart-ache or a head-ache. I have something far
worse. I have an *existence*-ache!"

Yorick could not contain his delight at this
new category. He gave Hamlet a big belly-laugh and
said:

"So long, young Prince, as you can say funny
things like that, you have not touched rock bottom—
and you never will."

Yorick and Hamlet got down on their hands
and knees and scooped out a big hole in the sand. One
by one they each gently placed three seagulls in the
hole. Then they pushed the sand back in and made a
grave for the birds. They stood up and stared down at
the little mound of sand.

"Shouldn't we say something?" asked Hamlet.

Yorick thought for a moment and then said

solemnly:

"We commit to the quiet earth our fellow mortals."

Hamlet now felt the need to say something as well:

"Dear Lord, forgive their *gullibility*."

Yorick smiled warmly at the lad. He was becoming more of a protégé for the jester than an heir for the King.

Hamlet found himself having to make his best and worst puns when he was most in pain. The Prince and Yorick walked down the coast. Behind them two dozen seagulls alighted on the pile of food scraps, hardly believing their luck, now that all the human beings had finally left. A few of the gulls clawed mechanically at the new grave.

The Skull of a Squirrel

A few days later, Hamlet could not get the dead seagulls out of his head and he decided he needed to talk to someone who was almost as lost in thoughts as himself. Prince Hamlet's best friend next to Yorick was a boy his own age called Horatio. He liked Horatio because he was also a bookworm who rarely ventured out into the world and could usually be found reading in the chapel inside the castle. When they came of age, Hamlet and Horatio were planning to attend a famous university in Wittenberg, in Germany, in order to study theology and philosophy. When Hamlet could not find Horatio in the chapel, he immediately went outside and made his way to the graveyard not far from the castle. He knew that Horatio took long walks, usually in circles, around the graveyard so he could think a thousand thoughts.

Sure enough, as Hamlet entered the graveyard, he saw Horatio on the other side of it and so he began walking along the circular path surrounding the headstones and crosses of wood shoved into the cold earth over all the dead Danes. The graveyard also had several trees in which one often saw black squirrels chasing one another or running in speedy circles around the trunk of a tree. Hamlet sped up and Horatio slowed down when he saw the Prince trying to catch up to him.

"I thought I would find you here," said Hamlet to Horatio.

"The graveyard is always empty and lets me think," returned Horatio.

"Empty except for the dead," observed Hamlet.

"They are no trouble to anyone, now. Their souls have departed. They are in Heaven."

"How do you know there *is* a Heaven"? wondered Hamlet. He was not so certain as his friend about the afterlife.

"The Holy Scriptures tell us so," replied a serene Horatio.

Hamlet knew he was supposed to believe this idea but his mind was too independent and often wandered off course. For a few minutes Hamlet and Horatio watched the black squirrels running in mad circles around the tree trunk. Finally, Hamlet said, "It seems to me that life and death are like those squirrels, always chasing each other."

"That is why," said Horatio, "we have heaven. Heaven is where the chasing ends and eternal afterlife begins."

"Do you *really* believe that?" asked Hamlet.

"I am most certain," said Horatio.

Hamlet wondered how someone could be certain about *anything*. Horatio was no doubt a clever boy but his piety struck Hamlet as lacking in imagination. What if Heaven is just a fairy-tale that adults cling to? Hamlet allowed his mind to chase itself in circles by asking these questions.

The two boys walked on the circular path around the cemetery in silence. In the distance a great, bulky figure and a smaller, slender one walked hand-in-hand towards them and Hamlet instantly recognised Yorick and Ophelia coming to the cemetery to join them. As they approached, Hamlet spied a small white object a few feet off the path. He dashed over to pick it up. It was the skull of a squirrel. As Ophelia and Yorick approached the two boys, Hamlet pitched the squirrel's skull into the big hands of Yorick, and said, "Can you make us laugh at *that*?"

Yorick had his audience of Hamlet, Horatio, and Ophelia, and he could see that his wit was being put to the test. Who could make anyone laugh about the death of a tiny creature, or any creature for that matter? They were surrounded on all sides by death. Yorick pondered the skull in his hands and began speaking, turning over the skull in his hands and in his mind.

"This might have been the skull of Reynard, the clever fox, but not so clever as to out-*fox* Death. Or this might have been the skull of a cat, who finished up its nine lives and could not avoid the *cat*-astrophe of Death.

The three children giggled at Yorick's awful puns. Even solemn Horatio allowed himself a bit of mirth as he contemplated the sad fact that Yorick was right in the sense that there is no heaven or afterlife for dead animals because they have no souls to begin with. At least that is what Horatio believed.

Ophelia gently chimed in at this point, "It's the skull of a *squirrel*, Yorick." The court jester's enthusiasm was undiminished, and he exclaimed:

"Alas, poor squirrel! This might have been the squirrel I used to watch chasing its own tail, racing around itself in tight little circles, a furry blur of black. Or this might be the black squirrel that portends a solar eclipse, as our Danish folklore tells us. Black squirrels are an ill-omen, I have heard. This poor chap has suffered the worst luck of all. Where is your bushy tail *now*, little creature?"

Yorick tossed the skull back to Hamlet, who contemplated it.

"Eclipsed forever!" said the Prince. "It makes you think."

Ophelia found her voice: "*Everything* makes *you* think!"

Yorick decided to add something to the mix: "Better to *laugh* than to think."

"But what's *funny* about death?" asked Hamlet.

They were walking in pairs now, Ophelia and Horatio strolling slightly ahead of Yorick and Hamlet. Twilight lengthened the shadows of the tombstones, as if to extend the cold domain of death.

Hamlet's question had reduced the others to silence.

Horatio turned his head and spoke up: "There's nothing funny about death. It is merely a transition to Heaven for good Christians. And a transition to other places for sinners."

Hamlet replied, "But what if you're wrong,

Horatio? What if death is not *anything at all*? What if we simply cease to exist? The evidence on the ground (he waved his hand at the graves) if not *under* the ground, is that we will be food for worms."

Ophelia replied, "Well, there's certainly nothing funny about *that*!"

The four walked in silence for a few more minutes. Horatio was stunned by the Prince's depressing views about death, but he did not know how to respond beyond simply repeating his own Christian beliefs. Finally, Yorick broke the silence. He knew he had to come up with something better than silly puns about foxes and cats. Yorick stopped walking and the three children faced him.

"To put it briefly, death makes life absurdly insignificant, and there's often something very amusing about that absurdity."

Hamlet instantly jumped in: "But I find the feeling of absurdity painful: it is like being mocked by life itself. It is absurd to suffer and endure hardship and complicated thoughts when it all adds up to—*nothing*. Seriously, Yorick, why get out of bed in the morning? What's the point?"

"There is no point," said Yorick, "except to *see what happens next*! The only way to deal with absurdity is to turn it into *curiosity*. And isn't it curious that we are the only animal who laughs, or *needs* to? We are absurdly curious and curiously absurd. We are seriously laughable and laughably serious. The only point of life is to throw things up into the air and see what happens. See how much you can juggle, just for the absurd pleasure of doing so.

Unless you plan to kill yourself, unless you plan *not to be*, then you are wasting your life if you don't laugh at absurdity all the way to the grave. Absurdity is absurd. It is a conjurer's trick to make you think life is supposed to have some grand meaning. Because life is absurd you should play with it, over and over, just to see how interesting and amusing you can make it. Being gloomy about absurdity is like living with one foot planted in your grave. Life is an absurd dance *because* death will snuff us out. If there were an eternity out there, it would only make our lives *more* meaningless, because only *it* would matter. The whole question of absurdity assumes some other kind of life outside of time that is not absurd. But if no such life exists, then the question of absurdity *is itself* absurd. It should not depress us or bedevil us. We should find it completely hilarious that we could be tricked into being so solemn by one absurd little word. We should smile away absurdity. We should laugh it into the grave. The only reason to live is to see what happens next and to try to *make* what happens next wonderfully exciting. Even making bad puns spices things up! And really good puns are like bursts of flavour in the mind. What more could you want?"

Hamlet and Ophelia began to giggle during this performance, but Horatio had a look of horror on his face, which made the other two children laugh even harder. Hamlet detected some inconsistencies in Yorick's argument, but Yorick was not trained in philosophy. And Hamlet saw that he veered away from what makes death funny in order to make sport with the idea of absurdity. It was altogether a slippery performance, but the question was impossible and they all knew it. Except Horatio. He thought everything that Yorick said was blasphemy and highly offensive. Horatio continued to believe that, for a good Christian, death was a promotion. For Hamlet, death was just silence.

As the four made their way out of the cemetery and back to the castle, Yorick turned them into a daisy-chain of dancers, all holding hands, and he sang a ballad. It was a song about the Grim Reaper harvesting people and dancing them to their deaths. But Yorick introduced variations and puns and turned around the sad story into a dance of life to celebrate every waking and walking moment as if it's your last, because it could be. Yorick was so joyous and witty that he beguiled the children from their sad thoughts. Even Horatio, although bringing up the tail of the formation and not wagging it very cheerfully, finally fell into step and could be heard laughing a little as they danced their way home.

Riding with the Queen

One week before the Christmas Court, the Queen decided Hamlet should go riding. The Queen was worried that Hamlet was spending too much time in the castle, often with annoyingly-clever Yorick and frightfully-serious Horatio. Both parents thought that he needed more fresh air and physical activity. The servants saddled up Hamlet's black horse, which he named 'Nightmare.' The Queen rode a beautiful white horse that Nightmare loved to chase.

And so it became a kind of game when Hamlet and the Queen went out for a ride. They would trot along together for half-an-hour and chat about the small things taking place at court, but then, without any warning, the Queen would suddenly stab her pretty shoes into the ribs of her horse and it flew down the path away from the castle. Before Hamlet could say anything, Nightmare would take off in pursuit. Nightmare was wonderfully fast and strangely determined to pursue the Queen's horse. Prince Hamlet held on for dear life, laughing and shouting encouragement and forgetting for a few precious moments to think about anything at all except catching his mother. How beautiful her long fair hair looked streaming behind her in the wind!

Eventually his mother would rein in her horse and allow Hamlet to catch it. The Prince would sidle up to his mother, both of them breathless, and they would laugh at their game of hunter and hunted. On this occasion, Hamlet's thoughts were not very happy, however, and he turned to a subject that was distressing him.

"Mother," he began, "I have dreams about you all the time. They are confusing. I don't know what they mean."

"You are such a curious boy," replied the Queen.

"Do you mean I am *inquisitive* or *odd*? The word 'curious' can mean both things."

"I suppose I mean both."

"I can see why," said Hamlet. "I am often a mystery to myself."

"You think too much for your own good. You think too much for anyone's good."

"That may be true—but how do you stop thinking? To me the mind is a flowing river that takes me along with it."

On this occasion, the Queen and Hamlet had ridden down to the coastline of Denmark. Seagulls were swooping and crying in the wind in their eternal search for the food that would let them live to swoop another day. The waves were crashing on the shore and receding back into the great, darkening sea. The sun was beginning to die in the sky and turned the water to a rich, copper colour, its choppy swells peaked like glittering diamonds. Hamlet and his mother stared at the sea and fell silent. Even their horses seemed to be mesmerised by the seascape and the rhythm of the waves.

"I think," said the Queen, "you need to start considering your position at court. After all, you will be the next King of Denmark. Isn't that enough to keep your mind busy?"

For the thousandth time in his short life Hamlet stared gloomily out to sea. He did not like this subject.

"Do you see those waves coming in?" he asked his mother.

"Of course I do."

"What happens to them?"

The Queen looked puzzled but then said, "They make a little swell and then they fall upon the beach."

"And then," said Hamlet, "millions more do the same thing. And will do so to the end of time."

"It's the natural way," replied the Queen, "I don't know what you're getting at."

"I think kings and kingdoms must be like those waves coming in. They rise up a little, make their pretty little curl and then crash and sink into the sand or else wash back out to start it all over again."

"You really are a *gloomy* little thing, aren't you," said the Queen and gave her son a rather hard look.

Hamlet could not look at his mother. Her words cut into him. Her stare hurt him. He loved her terribly and yet she was so unlike him. All his parents wanted to do was groom him to be King of Denmark. All he wanted to do was talk to them about his loneliness, his ideas, his beloved Yorick and about the endless enigma of death and what happens to us after we die. Hamlet simply could not understand why these subjects were not a thousand times more interesting and important than who commands a patch of dirt called 'Denmark.'

Hamlet turned to look at his beautiful, wind-swept mother. He gazed steadily into her ice-blue eyes and said, "You're right, of course, I *am* on the gloomy side." He realised that he would never be able to talk to his mother the way he talked to Yorick, to Horatio, and to Ophelia. She was too busy being a Queen to be much of anything else. This thought was another stab in Hamlet's heart but he was getting used to all the shocks the world gave him on a daily basis.

The horses began to paw at the wet sand as if they wanted more sport and, without any warning, Nightmare twisted around and bolted back towards the castle. It was the Queen's chance to chase her son and her white stallion lit out to follow the impetuous Nightmare. But the Queen did not want to outstrip the Prince and she let him stay a bit ahead of her as they raced back to the castle. Hamlet pretended that Nightmare had a mind of its own but in fact he had urged the horse to turn around and race for home.

The Queen and Hamlet dismounted and walked in silence together into the castle. The Queen bent down and gave the Prince a tiny kiss on his cheek.

"Good night, my dear, I must go see your father."

"Good night, mother," replied Hamlet, his voice as flat as a dead sea.

Hamlet walked through the castle back to his bedchamber. There, curled up on his pillow, he found his black kitten waiting for him. Hamlet called his kitten 'Inkling.'

[handwritten annotations in margins: "where did he kitten sudden", "one of the castle strays"]

When the kitten was curled up and purring in Hamlet's lap, or asleep on his chest and facing away from him like a Sphinx guarding the inverted pyramid of Hamlet's mind, the Prince was at leisure finally to be alone and think about what kind of day he had had. He would speak to Inkling as if it were a conscious creature who could understand what he said. Sometimes Hamlet was so lonely that he recited speeches to Inkling before falling into a troubled sleep. On this occasion, he formed his thoughts into a kind of poem, the kitten's purring creating a rhythmic music pulsing underneath Hamlet's meditations. The more Inkling purred, the more lyrical thoughts occurred to the pensive Prince.

Of all the Princes in the wide world

Why must I always be so gloomy?

Of all the brains to woman born

Why must mine be so roomy?

My mother is a splendid Queen, no doubt,

But she has no mind for me –

She thinks only of kings and things,

I think of *mortality*.

And yet I love her as truly

As any good son on this earth,

How could I fail to cherish

The woman who gave me birth?

Inkling opened its gleaming, emerald eyes, yawned, and fell back to its rich purring. Hamlet began to drift into sleep, a rare thing for him. He struggled to make one more verse to round off his day.

Sons and mothers–a curious affair,

In the one grows the other's beating heart–

Who could predict after a dozen years

What tidal forces will pull them apart?

Hamlet thought about the coming festivities at Christmas Court and decided to show his parents that he did have some talent—writing poetry, for example—even if they were not exactly the ones they wanted him to have. Inkling's steady purring was the last thing Hamlet heard as he fell into an unusually deep sleep, the sight of the Queen's blond hair lofting in the wind was the last image in his mind's eye before oblivion pulled him under.

talents

Christmas Court at Elsinore Castle

As the winter holidays approached, Prince Hamlet considered the important role he was to play in the Christmas court at Elsinore. The Queen had given her permission, knowing how much Hamlet enjoyed play-acting and playing with words. Hamlet loved to invent little dramas—he called them 'playlets'—and he was always looking for an audience. Sometimes members of the court would say, 'Hamlet has a playlet' and they would be summoned to see it performed.

Prince Hamlet slept even less than usual in preparation for his grand part in the celebration. The massive stone hearth in the Great Hall was piled high with logs that threw out lavish light on the assembled guests and on the players Hamlet had collected for the festivities. Iron candelabras as tall as sentries and lit with hundreds of candles stood along the walls of the Great Hall and huge wreathes of ivy clustered with bright red berries decorated the massive oak dining tables. At the top-table sat the King, the Queen, and Uncle Claudius. Prince Hamlet was seated by his mother. Ophelia and Laertes were next to Polonius. At the other tables the rest of the courtiers and the lords and ladies of Denmark were seated and feasting on wild game, their goblets brimming with wine and ale. Their laughter echoed throughout the Great Hall.

After two hours of feasting, suddenly young Hamlet sprang to his feet and turned to the King and Queen.

"It's time for some theatrical games...!"

Hamlet walked to the far end of the Hall, where Yorick was already waiting for him. Then Hamlet alone walked to the centre of the feasting tables, which had been arranged into a giant horseshoe. As he moved into a position to address his parents and all the guests, Hamlet transformed himself from a sad, rather drooping boy into a flamboyant Prince.

"Good to see him so high-spirited," said Gertrude to King Hamlet.

"He's fine so long as it's *play-acting*," replied the King.

Hamlet planted himself in the very centre of the Great Hall and when the King made motions with his hands, the guests eventually settled down and were quiet. They too had become accustomed to this yearly ritual and knew how important it was to humour Hamlet.

Hamlet waited for absolute silence and, staring directly at his mother, began his opening speech.

"Mother, Father, ladies and gentlemen of Elsinore, for this year's Christmas Court I have arranged for *four* separate entertainments..."

At this dire news, the King, Claudius and Polonius all groaned a bit, but a fierce look from the Queen sorted them out.

"We shall begin with our beloved court jester presenting a great feat of juggling. After that, Laertes and I will put on a Sword Play, followed by a Word

Play, followed by a poem I have composed for the occasion."

Polonius turned to Claudius, "The word *play* seems to be the key word."

"More wine!" roared Claudius, alarmed at this heavy menu of entertainment from the Prince.

Unable to restrain themselves, most of the guests erupted in laughter and quickly filled their glasses to fortify themselves. The Queen gave Hamlet a loving and reassuring look and her son continued.

"And now it's my pleasure to give you Yorick."

As Hamlet moved away from the centre of the Hall, Yorick came forward, dressed in a great green velvet cloak and a necklace of holly berries that Ophelia had woven for him. Yorick's hands were grasping several peculiar objects.

"King Hamlet, Queen Gertrude, assembled guests—the life of a court jester is not all pun and games. One often has to juggle many things at once to keep everyone happy, or at least amused."

Suddenly Yorick tossed a very pretty golden crown into the air and, as it reached the apex of its journey, the jester flicked the skull of a fox into the air. After the crown and the skull made a few rounds, Yorick launched an hourglass into the loop and juggled all three for a few moments before adding into the mix a dagger with a jewelled handle. Yorick's nimble hands became a blur as the crown, the skull, the hourglass and the dagger flew in a circle above him. Then Yorick produced a silver goblet and pitched it into the circle. Even the King and Claudius, no great fans of Yorick, had to admit this was a dazzling spectacle. Prince Hamlet stared at the five objects as if some kind of whirling puzzle were being presented to him. All at once, Yorick pulled a huge wing of roasted goose from his cloak and made it take flight to join the other objects pitched a good ten feet into the air to give him time to launch and re-launch them, as the guests cheered and applauded. But Yorick's act was not done.

With crown, skull, hourglass, dagger, goblet and goose wing arcing through the air, Yorick suddenly took the hourglass out of the circle and pitched it to young Hamlet, who caught it.

"There," shouted Yorick with great gusto, "I wanted you to see how time flies."

Then Yorick allowed the crown, the skull, the dagger and the goblet to come to rest in his hands and last of all the goose wing, which Yorick expertly caught in his upturned mouth. He approached the top table and firmly placed the skull in front of the King, the silver goblet in front of the Queen, the crown in front of Claudius and the dagger in front of Polonius. From Hamlet's point-of-view, the objects formed a beautiful still-life painting. He noticed that the Queen shifted uncomfortably in her throne when the crown was placed near Claudius, and she gave Yorick a look as black as Nightmare. The King did not appear to enjoy the skull that ended up in front of him. Polonius simply stared at the dagger and looked over at Prince Hamlet, who was—as usual—lost in thought.

With the goose wing still in his mouth, Yorick bowed deeply to the King and Queen and the guests laughed and applauded the court jester.

As Yorick passed by him, Hamlet said, "How did you manage to throw so much up into the air!"

"And into the *heir*," replied Yorick and smiled enigmatically at Hamlet, who resumed his position in the centre of the Hall.

"We have now arranged for sword-play," said the Prince.

"Finally, a bit of *action*! said the King. He would never know how his remark carved a permanent hole in his sad son.

At these words, young Laertes, brother to Ophelia, walked over to Hamlet and presented the Prince with a choice of two rapiers with the ends covered and blunted so they could not hurt anyone. Hamlet selected one of them. Laertes was a much more active and robust lad than Hamlet and it did not look like it would be a fair match. But the Prince had been practising for months in anticipation of the contest and he held his own as the two brandished their weapons and made more or less skilful lunges at each other. At one point, Hamlet made a particularly successful *riposte* and the Queen stood up and raised both her voice and her goblet of wine.

"The Queen drinks to Hamlet!"

Hamlet blushed at this outcry but was also deeply gratified by his mother's attention.

After another few minutes of feint-and-parry, the boys shook hands and received a polite pattering of applause from the court.

"At least he holds the sword at the right end," muttered Uncle Claudius, who was surprised that the usually passive Prince had any fighting skills at all.

Hamlet again assumed his position as impresario of the evening's entertainments.

"The centrepiece of our theatrical pieces is something I call *Word Play*."

quartet

King Hamlet, Claudius and Polonius all shifted uncomfortably in their chairs. They all thought that the Prince's fascination with words was becoming more than annoying and was misshaping his character into something too intellectual.

"This is a guessing game," announced Hamlet. "I will throw out questions and all of you try to figure out the answers."

The members of the Danish court shifted in their chairs and the wine and ale continued to flow.

"What do you say when a bear you have been hunting suddenly bolts and runs away?" asked Hamlet.

Hamlet looked around the court and was treated to stony silence. The King and Claudius exchanged hard looks. Surely the Prince wasn't going to make a silly joke about their bear hunt and how they all ended up in trees. After five long seconds, Hamlet turned to Yorick, who said, "The game's afoot."

"Correct" shouted Hamlet.

The Prince tried again.

"What is a device for tricking a woman into marriage?"

Silence all around. Yorick stared at Claudius,

who looked puzzled and busied himself with munching on a haunch of venison.

Hamlet again had to turn to Yorick.

"A spouse-trap!" exclaimed the court jester.

"Correct" said Hamlet and then he tried another riddle.

"What do you call a boy who is always under a black cloud?"

Hamlet waited patiently for someone in the court audience to say something. After a minute the lovely, small white hand of Ophelia fluttered like a dove into the air.

"Prince Hamlet" she said proudly.

Hamlet smiled and said, "You're very close." And for a moment his eyes rested on his dear friend who so wanted him to do well.

A few more moments passed before Yorick once again had to come up with the answer.

"An eclipsed son," he said.

"Correct!"

Hamlet decided to try some easier riddles.

"What do you call a goose that makes shocking noises at night?"

Looks of puzzlement and consternation all around until Ophelia finally made an effort.

"A poultry-geist!" she said, with great excitement.

"Correct" shouted Hamlet, delighted that

Ophelia had a mind to comprehend his own.

"But my dear Prince," objected Polonius, "That is such a low form of humour. Your puns of youth should grow a beard of solemnity."

Hamlet was not to be discouraged in his entertainments, but he did decide to speed things up and gave Yorick a look to suggest he wanted the answers to his riddles – and fast.

"What do you call twins before they are born?"

"Womb-mates" said Yorick instantly.

H: "And if the twins are buried together after death?"

Y: "Tomb-mates."

H: "And if the twins are melancholy together"

Y: "Gloom-mates."

H: "And what do you call a mind looking at itself in the mirror?"

Y: "A reflection."

H: "And what do you call people who are full of thoughts?"

Y: "Pensive."

H: "And if they love to go shopping because they don't have a single thought in their heads?"

Y: "Ex-pensive."

At this last jest, Ophelia giggled madly but clammed up when the rest of the court simply stared at her.

Hamlet had another dozen or so riddles in his head but decided to move to the last of the evening's festivities.

"And now," said the Prince, "I will conclude with a poem of my own making." The entire court, except for Ophelia, seemed to heave a huge sigh of relief at this welcome news.

"I call this poem," announced Hamlet, *The Prince of Cogitation.*

Laertes whispered to his sister, "What is *cogitation*?"

Ophelia replied, "It means 'to turn over in the mind.' Hamlet's mind tosses and turns like some great sleepless giant."

Hamlet stood dead-centre in the horseshoe of tables and addressed himself to the court, but mostly he made eye-contact with the King and the Queen throughout his recitation.

The Prince of Cogitation

Is it better to be loved or feared?

Now *that* is a Princely question

Is it better to be normal or weird?

There we have *my* obsession.

I cannot doubt that I am a Prince

And one day must play the King

Yet swords and warfare make me wince:

I prefer philosophy to any thing.

Making shishkebob out of Norwegians
Is not at all to my liking --
And why end up in hell's subregions
Because one has been a Viking?

Yorick, that dear wise old fool
Has given me odd thoughts to juggle –
And his merriment seems to overrule
Life's too-poisonous struggle.

I have therefore made use of cogitation,
Your pious postures to pester --
Hardly a great Dane at our celebration --
I am Denmark's *second*-best jester.

Hamlet waited for some applause but then shouted out his final line for the evening:

"Thus concludes our Christmas Court's ***feast-ivities*** for the night!"

The King groaned a general groan that spread throughout the court but Yorick gave Hamlet a hearty laugh and looked at the boy as if he were the son he never had, nor ever would have. As the court departed the Queen approached Hamlet and gave him a warm hug and said, "You ought to have been an actor."

Hamlet replied, "We are all actors, actually, and simply play our roles, unless the role doesn't fit."

The Queen, who understood little of her son's

mind, simply smiled and made her exit.

Yorick and Hamlet were left alone together in the Great Hall, a huge fire still raging in the fireplace, and a few dogs already asleep near where they sat.

"Yorick, do you think the evening was a success?" asked Hamlet.

Yorick thought that the entertainments had *not* been much of a success but he did not want to make an already dejected Hamlet any worse.

"I think," said Yorick gently, "that your mental playfulness is too much for most people."

Hamlet pondered this remark and then said, "Why do people dislike puns?"

"Many people say puns are the lowest form of humour," explained Yorick.

"But what do *you* think?" asked Hamlet.

"I think puns should put people under the spell of words. Puns conjure up two meanings from one word. That is a kind of magic."

Hamlet immediately brightened up.

"In other words," said Hamlet, very happy with himself, "Puns are a form of *wit-craft*."

Yorick smiled broadly. He loved the young Prince like no one else in the kingdom did.

"I think it was an excellent Christmas Court," said Yorick, "but now it's time for the Prince of Denmark to rest his young mind." Yorick walked Hamlet to his bedchamber and

It sounds like Yorick wanders to bed

Hamlet allowed the Prince to kiss him goodnight before wandering off to his bed to re-play all the night's events and to wonder about everyone's different reactions to his various entertainments.

He made a summary in his mind:

The Queen pretended to like my entertainments because she worries about my depression.

The King thought I was clever but he would rather I were a more normal boy who is better at the rapier than at rapier-wit.

Uncle Claudius was suspicious of my mind and wonders what mischief I am capable of.

Polonius sensed my intelligence but also thinks I am going to be hard to train up as a King.

Laertes is a well-meaning boy but cannot tell a moose from a goose.

Ophelia understands me telepathically and always wants me to do well. It's as if we beat together with one thinking heart.

And then Hamlet thought about the court jester. If I am ever lucky enough to marry Ophelia, thought Hamlet, Yorick will be not only my *best* man but my *jest* man.

And then the Prince tried to sleep. But his mind was racing, as always, and he fell asleep only after many hours of turning everything over and over again in his mind.

The Mystery of Death

A few weeks after the Christmas Court, Hamlet was sitting alone in the Great Hall and reading a book about cosmology. As he was becoming more and more lost in the starry heavens and how everything in the universe moves by invisible forces, he noticed the Queen slowly approaching him.

She sat down quietly across the table from him and did not say a word for a few long moments. Clearly something was wrong.

"Close your book," said the Queen.

Hamlet held his mother's gaze and closed his book.

"What's happened, mother—what's the matter?"

"I know you are an unusually sensitive boy and I don't want you to be too shocked," said the Queen.

"For heaven's sake, what's happened, mother?" said Hamlet with great anxiety, his eyes widening.

"And your attachment to him was also especially strong, and so…"

The Prince cut her off: "Please, mother, tell me what's going on!"

"Yorick is dead."

The Queen stared at Hamlet, her eyes

suddenly without any life or lustre, without warmth, like a doll's eyes.

Since he was two years old, Hamlet had never been at a loss for words. But now he was simply silent. His mother's vacant eyes were like black holes to fall into—and the young Prince fell and fell and fell, wordlessly, into her lifeless eyes.

Finally, Hamlet said, "Yorick is dead" but it was more of a question than a statement or acknowledgement.

"Dead, quite dead," said Gertrude, fearing the worst for her son's well-being.

Hamlet could not bear to look any longer into his mother's strangely dead eyes and so looked over at the great fireplace and the flames jumping around inside it.

"I saw him yesterday," said Hamlet, "and he seemed in fine health."

"People die suddenly all the time," said Gertrude, "in fact it's very common."

"But do we know *why* he died," asked Hamlet, confused by his mother's lack of grief about Yorick's death.

"Well, you know, Hamlet, he was only a court jester, so we did not look much into it. In fact, he is already buried. The physician said it might be something he ate. You know he would eat up half the kingdom if you let him."

Hamlet jumped to a conclusion: "Poison!" He looked straight at his mother.

Gertrude's eyes suddenly danced to life.

"Why do you say that?"

"Isn't it possible?" said Hamlet, his voice trembling.

"You mean food poisoning? Well, I suppose…"

"No, I mean food that *was* poisoned!"

Gertrude looked stunned and found herself saying:

"But who would ever want that silly court jester dead?"

Hamlet shot back, flinging the words at his mother with great force.

"He was *not* silly and he was my *best friend*!" screamed Hamlet and jumped up from the table.

Hamlet ran to his hiding place, pulled the heavy curtains behind him and quickly constructed his castle of big books so he could be completely alone to think and be miserable. Yorick suddenly dead! Why? Already buried! Why? His mother's behaviour had been extremely odd. Why?

Hamlet had heard about death mostly from his father who cheerfully told him of all the soldiers from other countries he had killed and of all the Danish soldiers who died heroically on the field of battle. But Hamlet had never seen death up close except for dead seagulls and all the other dead animals he would often come across on his long wanders outside the castle walls. The dead animals looked like they were sleeping, thought Hamlet, except they probably don't have dreams. What is death but sleep without dreams? It's simply a long sleep except you never wake up. Or, if there is a heaven or hell, you wake up there. But Hamlet doubted the whole business about heaven and hell. Yorick never talked about God or religion except to make a few jokes about fat friars and naughty nuns. But Yorick was such a good soul, then surely if there were a heaven, Yorick will have to get in. Hamlet struggled to imagine an eternal Yorick living forever in the afterlife. Would there be other court jesters in heaven? Would heaven be, for Yorick, as a reward, *nothing but* dead court jesters who had been brought back to life? Or, for a court jester, would heaven be a constantly applauding audience, wildly appreciative no matter what jokes one told? But what sense is there in *individual* heavens, tailor-made for us? And then what to make of eternity, where our pleasures are somehow extended for billions and billions of years? Wouldn't even the best pleasure become stale after a few thousand years, never mind billions of years?

Hamlet tried to imagine eternity. It was like trying to imagine infinity. Every time your mind approached a horizon a new horizon would appear. *Always. Forever.* The words made Hamlet's mind and stomach turn over and over and hurt. They already hurt because of the pain of losing his beloved friend. What could eternity possibly mean and how was it related to our mortality? If we are meant to live forever, then why do we have to die at all? It doesn't make any sense. That thought haunted Hamlet like a ghost lurking in the shadows of his mind.

All Hamlet knew for sure is that Yorick's death hurt him more than he had ever been hurt before. He had lost his best friend and his tutor in wit. Yorick was also the only one who would talk to him about the mystery of life and the even greater mystery of death. But with Yorick, no matter how depressing the subject, one could look straight into the deepest, darkest abyss and come away laughing. Yorick once told him that laughter was nearly the only way out of sadness. The only relief from grief was jesting. Hamlet could find nothing to jest about in Yorick's death. He wondered if he was ever going to get over it.

After three days of mourning, thinking, and being unable to speak to anyone, Hamlet decided to visit the grave of Yorick. He asked one of the servants to fetch his horse so he could make the short ride to the common graveyard where he had heard Yorick had been unceremoniously thrown into a hole in the earth. Why was he buried so quickly and without any funeral rites? Hamlet did not know.

When Hamlet saw Nightmare being led into the courtyard of the castle, he ran down from his room and quickly mounted the horse and rode to the graveyard. When he caught sight of the tombstone poking out of the black earth he felt an even stronger sickness and soreness in the pit of his stomach. No effort had been made to give Yorick an epitaph. Surely, thought Hamlet, a man as brilliant as Yorick deserves some kind of tribute on his gravestone. Hamlet pondered a number of things he might write on the tombstone. He thought it should be something a court jester might have written, something fanciful and whimsical, something that would laugh in the face of death. He stood there for long minutes pondering what to write as a final tribute to his dead friend. Hamlet considered writing the words:

HE THAT REMEMBERETH ME

SHALL NOT PERISH,

BUT HAVE EVERLASTING LAUGHTER

The grieving Prince also pondered writing:

BELOVED YORICK

HIS MIRTH IS NOW EARTH

Or

WHO'S LAUGHING NOW?

But the Prince finally decided to do something very simple.

Hamlet found a sharp stone and, kneeling down on the grave, etched a stark Y on the face of the tombstone. He shook in anguish as he pressed the stone into the larger stone. He made a short line and then a longer line touching it, like two scars meeting at an intersection. Hamlet then stood back a few feet and held up the lantern.

"Y" indeed, said the young Prince. Hamlet wondered about the plot of life if we all end up in a funeral plot.

To complete Hamlet's perfect misery, the sky opened up and a steady, cold rain began to fall. Hamlet looked up at the black Danish sky and allowed the rain drops to sting his face. He then rested his eyes once more on Yorick's gravestone before mounting Nightmare and, lashed by rain and grief, he raced to the cliffs overhanging a turbulent sea. He was struggling to get away from the death of Yorick but his thoughts were inescapable.

This was no ordinary mourning. This was no ordinary melancholy. It was as if the death of Yorick had given young Hamlet a permanent sense of loss and a genius for sadness. His mother would keep telling him it was just a phase he was going through. Hamlet thought of the phases of the moon, how it went from a pale roundness to a silvery sliver and back again. Yes, Hamlet thought, but it is always the moon during all its phases. Hamlet thought he was also like that: always changing but always the same, a gently glowing sadness with a dark side that no one else could see. It is not just a phase I am going through, he thought, it is who I am. I will never *not be* a sad lad. Just as the moon will always be the moon, growing or slendering, but always pale and haunting – the colour of ghost.

The faster young Hamlet rode his beloved Nightmare, the more he tried to forget the loss of Yorick. But the speed of his mind always outstripped any other kind of motion. No matter how he urged on Nightmare—through black forests, along perilous clifftops or on the coastline of Denmark near the dark green turmoil of the tempestuous sea—the image of Yorick stayed fixed in his mind's eye. Finally, the Prince allowed his exhausted horse to fall to a slow walk and Hamlet quietly made his way back to the castle. He made sure that Nightmare was well cared for and then he took his drenched and depleted body to his bed-chamber. As he climbed into bed, he recalled something Yorick had once said:

Once something has been pronounced dead you can be assured of its vitality.

Hamlet thought about this paradox and lay awake most of the night pursued by the relentless thought that the more dead he felt inside, the harder it was to sleep. He would never look upon anyone like Yorick again. He doubted his parents would hire another jester.

Hamlet on the Precipice

Prince Hamlet spent several weeks by himself, avoiding the company of all who claimed to know him. He shut himself off even from his mother. A word he had learned came back to him: *inconsolable*. It meant grief so deep that nothing could ever make you feel better again. It meant a sadness so hurtful in the heart that no one could say anything to make it go away.

There was only one person whom Hamlet might allow into his sadness, only one person who would not say something ridiculous to comfort him. His mother had disappointed him and had acted oddly in telling him about the death of Yorick. He loved his father but the King was someone who was too busy with affairs of state to care about Hamlet's strange grief over the death of a court jester.

And so when Ophelia discovered him in his sanctuary of books he recognised her soft footfalls but did not refuse her. She found him very much on his side of his fortification, walled in by words, as he often liked to be. She sat opposite him, quietly, and stared at the books separating them. He knew she was there but said nothing. There was nothing to say, not even to Ophelia, who shared a soul with him. Ophelia leant her head against the wall of books and did not speak a word. She wanted only to be close to her friend who had just lost his best friend in the world. What was there to say? After half an hour of silence, both Hamlet and Ophelia found themselves pushing through two upright books next to each other in the

Were

fortress. It was a kind of telepathy that made them do this at the same time. Hamlet gathered in his book and Ophelia took in the book he had pushed towards her. Now, there was a few inches gap in the wall of books, big enough to see through and speak through if they had wanted to. This had never happened before in all the many hours they had spent together in Hamlet's sanctuary.

Moments passed. Ophelia did not know what to do. Hamlet wanted more than anything to reach through and try to touch Ophelia but a greater part of him never wanted to touch anyone ever again. If you get very close to people they will die and leave you forever. What's the point of getting so close to something that will die? Ophelia knew Hamlet well enough not to intrude on his sorrow. After another five minutes of this silent agony, the Prince—who never made the first move—found his hand wandering into the gap left by the removed books. Ophelia peeked through the gap and saw his pale hand shyly crawling toward her and she let her own hand creep tentatively into the gap. The moment their fingertips met in the wall of books they stopped breathing. They each had fingers at the tips of words, words at the tips of fingers. Hamlet's heart was full to bursting because this was the Ophelia who dragged him out of the Reflecting Pond, the Ophelia who made him a crown of pansies, the Ophelia who wrote a song about how he would never be a proper Viking. And Ophelia felt in her keen friendship for Hamlet all the possibilities of blossoming love. But this was not the time. Each wanted to send the fortress of books scuttling across the stone floor of Hamlet's chamber. Closing their eyes, they felt the plush warmth of fingertips and the greater warmth of their growing telepathy. They said nothing. They caressed each other's fingertips for a few precious moments and Hamlet nearly forgot about the death of Yorick. Hamlet breathed a sigh, Ophelia a moan. After a minute or two Ophelia pulled back her hand and left the bedroom. Hamlet was at first startled and nearly pushed his hand all the way through the gap in the wall of books. But then he understood. Ophelia knew there was nothing she could do for this kind of pain. This was sadness that physical intimacy could not touch. Hamlet loved her all the more for knowing that.

The Prince put on his heavy cloak, left the castle and walked out on his own for many miles until he reached the cliffs overlooking the great, dark sea. All around him the crying seagulls were circling and swooping in their endless quest for food. Sometimes the gulls would feed on the sand crabs on the shore. Occasionally a hawk would dive down and astonish a gull with its talons and whisk it off, both shrieking, the one in triumph, the other in terror, the one to eat and the other to be eaten even before its tiny, pumping heart had stopped.

Everything, thought young Hamlet, wants to kill and eat everything else. Nature is predatory. But my father is no different. He always wants to kill his way to a bigger kingdom even as he tries to avoid being swallowed by the kingdom next door.

Hamlet began to talk to himself, a habit he was beginning to develop when he found himself alone with his very wordy mind.

"Nature," said Hamlet to the sky, to the waves, to the crying seagulls, "is everything trying to eat everything else. But the kingdom of Denmark is also a kind of predator as it tries to conquer other kingdoms. On the battlefield all the slain soldiers are picked at by the crows while the dead bodies are fresh, and further devoured by other birds of prey when the bodies are rotten carcases. Finally, the decaying body becomes a picnic for worms. And then an old beggar comes along and uses one of those worms to catch a fish. When the beggar eats the fish he is eating a tiny bit of the dead soldier still trapped in the worm still trapped in the body of the fish. The circle of life is the same thing as the circle of death."

"But the mind feeds only on *itself*" exclaimed Hamlet, with some satisfaction. He thought how much Yorick might have liked that turn of phrase, that turn of mind, and he stared out to the incoming waves. Poor Yorick was dead. He will *never never never* be here again, Hamlet thought miserably. And then a truly terrifying thought occurred to him. If life and death are bound in the same endless circle, like waves that swell and break and die upon the seashore, forever and ever, only to be replaced by new rising and falling waves, for eternity, then *what's the point of living*? If we end up as a meal for worms, or like wasted waves, leeched into the sand, then why go on living? It was a terrible, true question. Nothing was more terrible or true.

Prince Hamlet moved closer to the very edge of the cliff and looked down. One more step and he would fall a great distance onto the rocks below and then be swept into the sea and eventually taken out with the tide. Hamlet imagined how his body and his brain, now drowned, dead things, would be fed upon by sea-creatures. It was too awful to think about but Hamlet could not stop thinking about it. Hamlet leant into the wind that was rising fiercely from below and was keeping his body from toppling head-long into the churning, black sea. Hamlet closed his eyes and put his arms behind his back and clasped his hands. Suddenly, he heard a single gull crying a few feet out in front of him, as if waiting for the young prince to fall forward so it could begin picking at his mangled but fresh corpse on the shore below. Hamlet opened his eyes. The seagull was waiting for him to fall to his death. Hamlet's mind swirled with thoughts of his stern father, Ophelia's twilight eyes and pale petal-like hands, his beautiful but occasionally distant mother and his beloved Yorick, already mouldering in the cold earth.

Hamlet thought of the letter Y he had scratched on the headstone. The seagull cried more sharply but it sounded almost like a peal of laughter.

Suddenly he remembered something Yorick once told him. Hamlet and the jester had been having one of their philosophical discussions and he had asked Yorick what the purpose of life was.

"If we are to die anyway", asked Hamlet, "then why go on living?"

Yorick scratched his bald head and thought about the question for a long time. A mysterious smile spread across his face and then Yorick said:

The only reason to stay alive is... to see what happens next.

Yorick's reply swirled like a small sea in the shell of Hamlet's ear. Yes, thought Hamlet, if you die then your simple curiosity dies with you. You don't get to see the future. You don't get to see *anything*— ever again. You don't get to read or think or race to the reflecting pond through the wildflower meadow. You never get to see how the sun and the moon rose in Ophelia's eyes. Or to hear her soft voice in beautiful conversation. And when you die you never get to use your mind again. Although Hamlet knew that his mind was often a torment to him, he also knew that he had a really good mind, full of playful words and interesting ideas and sparkling bits of wit. Yorick had once said to Hamlet:

You must play with life so that life doesn't play with you.

Hamlet thought: It is not just pulling a rabbit out of a hat—it is pulling *existence itself* out of a hat. That is the ultimate hat-trick to stay alive.

Hamlet turned from the steep precipice and the strange seagull and the black sea and he began to walk slowly but steadily towards the castle, whose honey-lights in the windows gave him comfort as he made his way along the steep path leading home. When he arrived in the Great Hall he found his mother waiting for him and, although he was nearly thirteen years old, she took him to his bed chamber. Having helped him into his huge bed, the Queen kissed him on his forehead and said, "Good night, sweet Prince. Sleep well." She floated gracefully out of the room. Hamlet tried to sleep but his fighting heart kept him awake for a long time. Yorick was gone forever but somehow alive whenever the young

Prince played with words. At last sleep closed in on Hamlet and his troubled spirit rested in the silence of the castle. Hamlet awoke at midnight, or he thought he awoke, to the sound of Yorick's laughter. He quickly sat upright in his bed. He heard the laughter again, this time closer. Hamlet peered into the darkness and waited, his heart thumping harder and harder. Could Yorick be haunting him?

Thrilled by the chance that Yorick's ghost might be out there trying to talk to him, Prince Hamlet lay awake the rest of the night, wrapped up in thoughts of ghosts. As pale, pink light began to glaze the white walls of his bed-chamber, Hamlet thought he heard Yorick's voice coming from behind his door. Two words hung in the air and then tapered off into silence.

G o o o o d   m o o o o r r r r n n i n n g...

Hamlet caught his breath and listened more intently than ever. Was Yorick wishing him a 'good morning'? It seemed too simple and easy. Then the ghost or spirit or whatever it was spoke again, this time only the second word, and drew it out in the middle so that it was deeper and the long vowel sound reverberated throughout his room. There was a long pause as Hamlet's heart and brain raced with excitement. Then the second word was repeated one more time, with the long *o o o o o* sound strangely accented. It sounded just like:

m o u r n i n g.

Suddenly Prince Hamlet understood. It was Yorick's voice. It was just like Yorick to play with words from beyond the grave. Hamlet heard no more of the voice and eventually fell back to sleep and awoke to a room flooded with strong light. Hamlet sat up again in bed. Was it a dream or ghost, he wondered? Or a ghost *in* a dream? Or the ghost *of* a dream? Or the *dream* of a ghost? Hamlet ran through the possibilities, but he could not deny that voice and those two words that would haunt him for the rest of his life.

What Happens Next

Later that morning, Prince Hamlet vaulted from his bed, threw on some clothes and dashed to the Great Hall and found the King, the Queen, and Uncle Claudius still at breakfast. Hamlet stood in front of the three of them, more lighthearted than they had seen him for a long time. He had been in mourning for weeks and weeks and they had not seen him in a good mood for ages.

"You look well this morning, young Prince," said the Queen cheerily.

"I have undergone a transformation," replied Hamlet.

"Indeed, that *is* good news," said the King.

"I shall no longer pay so much attention to my bad dreams and to my unconscious mind," said Hamlet.

"That would seem a wise thing to do," added Uncle Claudius. "Your dreams seem to get the better of you."

"No, I won't pay attention to my unconscious mind—I have found something better to do!" exclaimed Hamlet.

"And what is *that*?" asked the King.

"I have decided," said Hamlet, "to pay attention to something else."

"Well, what is it?" asked the Queen impatiently.

"Yes, what *is it*?" asked Claudius impatiently.

Hamlet said with great passion:

"I have decided to pay attention to my pun-conscious mind!"

And with that the young Prince danced around madly in front of the three astonished adults, repeating the words, with great merriment, "my pun-conscious mind! -- my pun-conscious mind! -- my pun-conscious mind!"

"And *that's* the next King of Denmark?" said Uncle Claudius, throwing a doubtful look at the Queen and King.

"Well," said the King staring in disbelief at his son, "at least we won't have to replace Yorick."

The Queen looked at her capering, frolicking son and thought to herself that he would no longer be sad and lonely, so long as he had words to play with.

Hamlet ran off to his secret nook and spent the rest of a very good morning reading and thinking about words. He continued to wonder what kind of king he would make when the time came. He looked forward to being sent off to study philosophy and theology at the University of Wittenberg in Germany. He had heard stories of a professor there called Doctor Faustus who was reputed to have a study with thousands of books in it, piled from the floor all the way up to the ceiling. He must be a *King of Words*, thought Hamlet, and just the kind of ruler I would like to be when I grow up.

Hamlet decided to share his new cheerfulness with Ophelia. He wondered if she might be a little weary of his dark and melancholy moods. He looked all over the castle but could not find her. Finally, he went outside of the castle and began to prowl around to see where she might be. He eventually wandered to the graveyard where he spent so much time. He found Ophelia at Yorick's gravesite, staring in sorrow at the big Y Hamlet had etched on the gravestone.

"The fair Ophelia!" Hamlet sang out, "Why are you here?"

"Why, indeed," said Ophelia, pointing at the marking on the gravestone.

The two children stared ponderously at the Y.

Hamlet had told Ophelia about his theory that Yorick might have been poisoned. Ophelia agreed that both the Queen and Claudius were unhappy with Yorick for some reason. As the two children stood staring in disbelief at the Y, Hamlet's good mood began to sag but then he remembered something Yorick had told him.

"Do you know what the purpose of life is?"

Ophelia sadly shook her head from side to side. Hamlet and Ophelia had often discussed such deep questions. Ophelia had come up with an idea he had never thought of. She once told him that if our lives are preoccupied with eternity, then our lives here and now were completely meaningless. All meaning was in the future, never in the present. Ophelia had said to him, "Better to make a heaven on earth than wait around to die and go to a heaven that is someone else's idea of perfection." Hamlet thought this was a mighty profound thing to say.

Ophelia had been considering Hamlet's question and finally said:

"What if the purpose of life is to transcend the need to ask the question?"

Hamlet was struck dumb, which almost never happened. He could only think to ask Ophelia to explain a bit further, which she did.

"What if instead of worrying about the WHY of life and what gives life meaning, we become Godlike by not needing a WHY anymore? Interestingly, that would also make us into healthy animals again, who never ask WHY about their existence. They simply live and they live simply."

Hamlet was happy Horatio was not around to hear this thought, because he would have said it was blasphemous. The Prince likened Ophelia's mind to a rare rose that blossoms unseen, but that she sometimes shared with him. And he wondered if her thoughts had already written his. They were that close. It was as if a magic wand were turning the pages of one mind. Although they were often solitary children, they also considered themselves—as they liked to put it—"alone together."

Hamlet suddenly recalled Yorick and what he had said about life.

"Do you know," said Hamlet, "what Yorick said about the purpose of life?"

Ophelia did not know. Hamlet took her delicate hands in his and looked deeply into her twilight blue eyes.

"The purpose of life is...*to see what happens next!*"

Ophelia slowly took on board these five words and her face began to brighten.

"And what," she shyly asked the young Prince, "is going to happen next?"

"How about a game of chess?

Ophelia's sad face lit up instantly.

"I accept."

And the two children walked on light feet back to the castle, holding hands, their fingers braided together.

Ophelia did not know that Hamlet had spent half the night outside the castle, carving a set of ice pieces, just as Yorick had done for him months earlier. When they reached the castle, he asked Ophelia to stoke up the fireplace while he disappeared for a few minutes to fetch the same pouch Yorick had used to store the chess pieces. Hamlet ran off to collect the chess set and when he returned he quickly poured out the pouch onto the table, to the surprise and delight of Ophelia, who intuitively guessed the meaning of having the pieces made of ice.

"Yorick knew you well," said Ophelia.

Yorick had also taught Ophelia how to play and, like Hamlet, she seemed more intrigued by evolving patterns on the board than by winning. For the first few minutes the chess pieces created a mirror image of each other, an accelerating battle of wits as the melting pieces forced the players to pick up speed. Against all his wishes and desires, Hamlet was forced to deploy his Queen and push her into possible peril.

As increasingly beset chess pieces began to weep water onto the board, Hamlet and Ophelia went on the attack and many slippery knights, bishops, and castles were taken off the board. As endgame approached, both Queens had to be sacrificed, to the great horror of Hamlet. At this point the children began to push pawns to try to retrieve the lost Queens. Ophelia thought to herself: If you push the pawn far enough, you get to be a Queen. She considered the analogy to her own position in the court of Denmark, where she was, essentially, a pawn.

Ophelia was successful in getting her pawn to the other side of the board and she happily exchanged the pawn for her Queen. Before Hamlet could get his own pawn across the board, Ophelia went on the attack, captured his eager pawn and succeeded in pinning down Hamlet's last remaining piece, his black King. Ophelia had both her Queen and King remaining on the board but no other pieces. She finally outflanked the black King so that, although he was not in check, he had no place to go.

Hamlet conceded that the game was a stalemate and he said so.

Ophelia could not resist: "May *we* never become stale mates."

"Mais oui" replied Hamlet, who knew a little French.

Hamlet came around to Ophelia's side of the great oak table and sat very close to her, facing her on the wooden bench. The young Prince gently said to her, very quietly, "I have written a sonnet for you, about you, about us."

Hamlet knew the sonnet by heart and recited it for Ophelia, falling into her eyes as he spoke.

We two had love at first conversation,

And when into my reflection I fell

You pulled me out of vexed cogitation

And put me under your beguiling spell.

For six months our minds were feathered by love,

And our young thoughts delighted to take wing,

Making intellectual heavens above

Of which Plato first taught us all to sing.

The thoughts I start you finish in your soul,

As our mental marriage becomes an art,

Written on our heart's voluminous scroll,

Its beauty unrolls until death do us part.

Pondering together from womb to tomb,

Our kindred souls awake in constant bloom.

Ophelia listened in wonder as Hamlet recited the poem. The final couplet made her heart flower and gave her an idea.

"To the Reflecting Pond!" she exclaimed with great excitement. She had been working on her weaving technique and wanted to make her friend another pansy-crown along the way. Hamlet did not need any urging. Immediately the two set out for their favourite place in the entire kingdom of Denmark. Their hearts buoyant, they were alone together, enjoying the seriousness of children at play.

On the table, the ice-queens drooped until their carved crowns sat in tiny puddles of water. The chess pieces would be gone by the time Hamlet and Ophelia reached the willow-swept pond.

The End

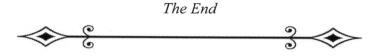

Hamlet in 665 words

If you have never read or seen Shakespeare's longest and most famous play, or if you need to give your memory a good kick in the trousers, then the following plot summary may help.

At some point in the 16th-century, the Prince of Denmark, called Hamlet, returns home from Wittenberg (nest for both the real Martin Luther and the fictional Doctor Faustus) to attend the funeral of his father the King, also called Hamlet. He has been told that a snake bit his father. He returns to the castle in Elsinore, Denmark. Only two months after the funeral, his mother the Queen, called Gertrude, marries Hamlet's uncle Claudius, the only brother of the dead King. Prince Hamlet is not at all pleased by the speed with which his mother sailed from his wonderful father, the dead King, to his dodgy Uncle Claudius.

Hamlet's girlfriend, Ophelia, is told by both her brother (Laertes) and her father (Polonius) to ignore Hamlet's love for her. Hamlet knows nothing of their advice and thinks Ophelia is just being fickle, which reminds him of his mother's weakness in going from one man to another.

The Ghost of the dead King tells Prince Hamlet that Uncle Claudius poisoned him so he could become King. Hamlet appears ready to be an avenging son who will push a knife into Claudius to repay his father's murder but he finally takes his time, either because he is a coward and lacks the nerve to do it or because he wonders if the Ghost is telling the truth. Hamlet also decides to be a bit of a clown/fool in order to make the court keep guessing what's troubling him so much.

Hamlet devises a play-within-a-play to determine if Claudius is in fact guilty. The Prince twice stages a scene very much like the murder reported to him by the Ghost. It works. Claudius runs off to confession and Hamlet nearly kills him while he is praying but decides to wait until a more appropriate time when the King is not trying to save his soul.

In confronting his mother about her infidelity, Hamlet kills the spying Polonius, <u>wishfully</u> thinking it is the King. Not happy about his murderous nephew, Claudius banishes Hamlet from Denmark to England, where he has contrived that his nephew will be killed the moment he makes landfall. Hamlet turns things around so that his boyhood pals and his escorts to England (called Rosencrantz and Guildenstern) are the ones put to death the moment they get to England. Hamlet returns to Denmark, much to the surprise and alarm of the guilty King.

Driven to despair and probably to madness by Hamlet's murder of her father, Ophelia drowns in a river but it is not clear if it is a suicide. Prince Hamlet finds himself in the very graveyard where his girlfriend is soon to be buried. Before her body arrives, the gravedigger churns up a skull that just happens to belong to Hamlet's best friend, the former court jester, called Yorick. Hamlet fondly remembers his friend but is horrified by how everyone we love ends up as dirt and dust. It makes all life seem meaningless and absurd. Even Caesar and Alexander the Great end up as dirt. That fact intensifies Hamlet's melancholy.

and/or

Fearing Hamlet's possible madness and his ability to murder, Claudius and Laertes plot to kill Hamlet by poisoning both a cup (or and) the tip of a sword that Laertes will use in a sword fight with Hamlet.

In the final scene of this tragedy, Hamlet agrees to sword play with Laertes (who is trying to avenge his dead father, Polonius) where two kinds of poison are waiting for him. His mother accidentally drinks from a poisoned cup to toast her son's success and she dies, telling Hamlet she has been poisoned. Laertes gets his own poisoned sword stuck into him and he also dies, blaming the King as he expires. Also touched by the poisoned sword, Hamlet, with only minutes to live, finally kills Claudius. Denmark is overrun by troops from Norway and a new ruler, Fortinbras, installs himself. Hamlet is carried off stage as if he is a soldier.

Hamlet is called 'The Melancholy Dane' because of his habit of sadness. And he is considered to be the most complex and intellectual character ever to be put on stage. Shakespeare wrote Hamlet *in 1601 and the play has been enormously popular ever since.*

Discerning readers and lovers of the play will notice that I have slightly ignored the rather baffling fact revealed by the Gravedigger that Hamlet is thirty years old, and thus by the time Prince Hamlet is twelve, Yorick would have been for dead for five years. I have kept Yorick alive for another five years to befriend and mentor Hamlet. Since most readers and viewers think of Hamlet as being about 19-23, I hope I shall be forgiven my literary opportunism.

About the Author

J P Söderholm is currently working on a second children's book called *The Grammar Ghost*. He is also evolving a book on hands, a book of dialogues (mostly with former students) entitled *Of Two Minds*, and a memoir called *Limping After Lord Byron*. He lives in London.

Works by J P Söderholm

Fantasy, Forgery and the Byron Legend (The University Press of Kentucky, 1996).

Beauty and the Critic: Aesthetics in an Age of Cultural Studies (The University of Alabama Press, 1997). Edited collection, with an introduction by the editor.

Byron and Romanticism: Essays by Jerome J. McGann (Cambridge University Press, 2002). Edited collection, includes a dialogue between McGann and the editor.

Platonic Occasions: Dialogues on Art, Literature and Culture, with Richard Begam (Stockholm University Press, 2015)

Recently Conceived: Essays from the Langton, Editor (Langton Press, 2015).

Great Apes: A Shrewdness of Poetic Imitations and Other Follies, with Ken Moffat (Langton Press, 2015).

Hideous Progeny: Bicentenary Essays on Mary Wollstonecraft Godwin's Frankenstein, Editor (Langton Press, 2016)

Website:

http://www.dialogicimaginations.co.uk/

Printed in Great Britain
by Amazon